7 BENEFITS OF FIAS FOR RETIREMENT

RETIREMENT IS A ROLLERCOASTER. ARE YOU PREPARED TO ENJOY THE RIDE?

SEAN A. RUGGIERO CEP, RICP®, WMCP®

INVESTMENT ADVISOR REPRESENTATIVE

Published by Mindstir Media, LLC
45 Lafayette Rd | Suite 181| North Hampton, NH 03862 | USA
1.800.767.0531 | www.mindstirmedia.com

Printed in the United States of America

ISBN-13: 978-1-7372-791-3-6

Dedicated to my family, Charissa, Charles, Tyson, Marcus & Lola

Special thanks to all the agents, advisors, managers, coworkers, and organizations who helped me along the way.

Contents

INTRODUCTION

The Retirement Rollercoaster

Imagine you are on a rollercoaster. The slight nervousness when you are in line waiting to board. The feeling of anticipation as you "clank, clank, clank" your way up to the top of the first peak, and then the rush of adrenaline as you accelerate through a feeling of freefall down the rails, followed by a jarring hard left turn followed by a jarring hard right turn. All this to stimulate your sense of danger and to create a true "thrill ride." The enjoyment of a rollercoaster can only be achieved when you know and trust that you are safe throughout the entire experience. If there was ever any doubt that you were safe, you wouldn't even think about riding.

Retirement for many Americans can be like a rollercoaster. We experience the ups and the downs, the jarring turns, and the panic-inducing plummets. However, we have no guarantees and no trust that we are going to be taken care of, so it creates fear and not enjoyment. Is that how we want our retirement to go? Does this sound like a "fun ride"?

Fortunately, you have a choice how you want to experience retirement. For most of us, we don't want it to feel like a rollercoaster, and for good reason! For those who want to feel some of the ups and not the downs, there is a solution, and that solution is a *Fixed Indexed Annuity*.

I know, I know. "An annuity?" is what many of you might be thinking, but I have found over my last fifteen years that when most Americans think of an annuity, they are either thinking of a lifetime income annuity, or the infamous variable annuity, which is maligned (in many cases rightfully so) for its high fees and market risk. No, I am talking about a different annuity, a rather newcomer to the game. I am talking about the Fixed Indexed Annuity, or *FIA*. Renowned finance professor and award-winning author, Moshe Milevsky said it best when he said, "saying you don't like annuities is like saying you don't like funds without clarifying what funds you are talking about; mutual funds, hedge funds, index funds?" So, if you're saying you don't like Fixed Indexed Annuities, then I challenge that you don't truly understand them, or you've been given some bad advice.

But wait! Pump the brakes! My number one goal is to help you in creating a retirement plan. Secondly, it is to introduce to you the Fixed Indexed Annuity. I'm not here to sell you an annuity or sell you anything. Most important to me is that you work to develop a plan and educate yourself on the challenges that are ahead and the tools you have at your disposal, including an FIA.

It is important to point out that I am an Investment Advisor Representative, and I *can* advise clients to purchase securities (stocks, bonds, mutual funds, etc.) as well as annuities, which are an insurance product. I believe that the right securities have their place in retirement in the right situation. I also believe that the stock market, specifically low-cost index funds, are the best way to build wealth while accumulating money for retirement, but an FIA is the single best product I've seen when it comes to conquering all the challenges that we face in retirement. This book is not specific financial advice, because everyone's situation is different, and everyone's needs are different. This book is about education and inspiration. The education to have confidence in making a decision, and the inspiration to optimize your retirement and enjoy what you've worked hard to obtain. So, leave the rollercoaster for the amusement park and hop aboard a more enjoyable and well-planned retirement!

A Failing Grade

According to TIAA-CREF, Americans spend less time planning for their retirement years than choosing a restaurant or their next flat screen TV purchase. Funny? I don't think so. Scary? Yes, especially when you consider all the retirement challenges that Americans face today. If we take a moment to really reflect on this, we can discover how this happens.

As young Americans, we start by going to school in the hopes of getting a "good" job. While working, we keep our nose to the grindstone and try to take advantage of the company 401k and save along the way for retirement, which always seems like some distant dream we will never actually get to. Before we know it, we are there, and we are supposed to make some of the most impactful decisions of our lives without any education. These retirement decisions will affect the next three decades of how we live, and we've done nothing to prepare for it.

Is it really our fault? I have often wondered why there isn't a more practical curriculum taught in school. A class where we learn about credit scores, mortgages and yes, retirement savings and spending. How to plan for retirement, and just as important, how to execute that retirement. So, I don't blame any individual for being underprepared for retirement, but I do believe that it's your job and your job alone to fix that, so reading this book can go a long way to resolve this problem.

As mentioned before, I am going to introduce you to something called a Fixed Indexed Annuity, or FIA. This is an annuity that is the fastest growing annuity in existence today, but probably the least understood. It is more than just a longevity hedge, and it is not the fee-heavy variable annuity which has given the annuity word such a black-eye. I ask you to keep an open mind and read this book with the intention of learning more and I promise you will finish the book more prepared and more confident in your retirement, regardless of if you implement an FIA.

Ask Yourself, Are You A Saver or An Investor?

Have you ever heard someone say "I am investing for retirement?" No, it just sounds wrong. The saying goes "I am saving for retirement." As I have worked with thousands of clients, directly and indirectly, over the past 15 years, I have learned that most "Middle Americans," those that have $100,000 to maybe $1,000,000 set aside for retirement, are savers, not investors. Why do I say that? Simply put, your average American doesn't tolerate risk well.

Investors understand the trade-off of risk versus reward. Investors are willing to lose some money in the hopes that they will eventually gain more later. Investors normally invest with money they are willing to lose. Those are the hallmarks of a true investor. In my experience, most Americans are not investors. Most of us panic when our investments start to lose money. In fact, there is a whole category of investment philosophy called "odd lot" investing. The "odd lot" investment strategy banks on individual investors (those who usually buy odd lot shares, i.e. less than 1000–10,000 shares at a time) are inevitably going to be wrong. This means that, if "Mr. Smith" who has $20,000 to invest, decides to buy or sell 20 shares of XYZ corporation stock, he is usually doing it for the wrong reason! This phenomenon wouldn't hold true if the average "Middle American" was truly an investor.

So, ask yourself again, are you an investor or a saver? Investors are tolerant of risk, comfortable losing money, willing to leave funds exposed to market risk to ride out market down swings. Does that describe you?

Savers are just that, saving money, or setting funds aside from their paychecks in the hopes of one day retiring. Savers like to see a steady and compounding growth of their retirement nest-egg, and if their account goes down, they react with panic and usually sell at the wrong time. Is that you? Do you feel sick at the prospect of losing 10% or 20% of your retirement nest-egg? If so, don't worry, you are not alone. In fact, you are in the majority of Americans. Of the thousands of clients I've worked with over the past 15 years, I have met very few who were actually investors, regardless of how they described themselves.

This book is for the many American's today who realize they have numerous retirement challenges that their parents didn't have. This book is for those retirees, or those preparing for retirement, who consider themselves savers first, investors second. It is also (and I am happy to deliver this news) for those people who haven't defined themselves or developed any retirement plan whatsoever! This book has been written to provoke thought and help Americans with their retirement plan, whether they have spent any time preparing previously or not.

Each of the *Seven Benefits of FIAs* (that is a Fixed Indexed Annuity) is a benefit to you, the reader. My goal is for each reader of this book, regardless of their unique situation, to learn more about their retirement and how to best protect, grow, and enjoy that which they have worked decades to build.

I want to sincerely thank you for taking the time to read this. It is an honor to share it with you and I want you to know that if you have any questions, I'll do my best to answer them and I can be contacted at sean.ruggiero@safemoneysmart.org

CHAPTER 1

RETIREMENT CHALLENGES TODAY

80 Years of Change

Today's Americans are facing more retirement challenges than they have in the past 80 years. The decline of pensions, low bond yields, longer lifespans, restrictions in Social Security, inflation, cost of long-term care, rising health care costs, market volatility, and pandemic disease have all combined to create seemingly insurmountable retirement challenges for many Americans today.

80 years ago, Americans were amid the Second World War. From an economic standpoint, the World War was a massive boon for America. The American industrial engine was essentially responsible for winning the War, and the economy and its workers benefited from it nationwide.

When the GIs came home from the war, there were more opportunities than ever before, with high paying jobs, new homes, and home loans available, and those who worked for their company could anticipate a low chance of being laid-off with the best health benefits available and a knowledge that they would be able to retire with a pension for them to live out their days happily.

Social Security was fully funded and there were still sixteen workers for every benefit recipient. When combined with their pensions, there was little need for additional investments in the stock market, and that was left to the rich who wanted to explore some riskier investments.

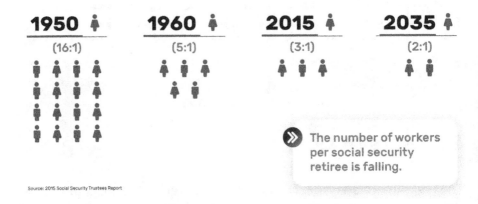

The Population is Aging

1950	1960	2015	2035
(16:1)	(5:1)	(3:1)	(2:1)

The number of workers per social security retiree is falling.

Source: 2015 Social Security Trustees Report

Fast forward to today. Almost all pensions offered by corporations are gone. Social Security is underfunded, and retirees must rely on funding their own retirement through defined contribution plans, such as a 401k, 403b, or 457 plan. The graph below shows the steep decline in pensions since 1980. A trend that continues to this day.

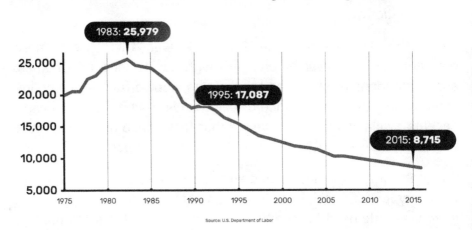

Number of pension plans with 100 or more participants

1983: **25,979**

1995: **17,087**

2015: **8,715**

Source: U.S. Department of Labor

This shift from pensions to defined contribution plans has swelled the volume of stocks being traded on an annual basis, and it has also left Americans' retirements tied to the performance of these underlying market investments. The graphic below illustrates how drastically the percentage of Americans invested in the stock market has changed over the past six decades.

Percentage of Americans who own Stocks

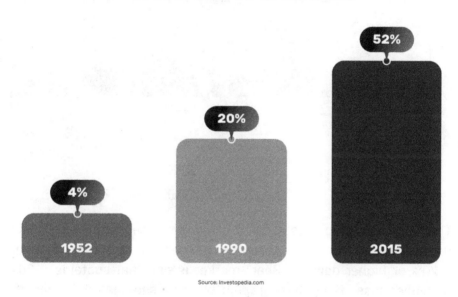

Source: Investopedia.com

Having one's retirement dependent on the performance of the stock market is a challenge that many of us didn't see coming. Being aware of it and planning accordingly is the first step in preparation.

Market-Driven Retirement

When a retirement is tied to the market performance, it is obviously vulnerable when there is a market downturn. If we look at the Standard & Poor's 500 (S&P 500) which tracks the top 500 companies by capitalization in the United States, we see that the market is a continuous series of "Bull" and "Bear" markets. Statistically, the market has gone up 73% of the time since 1970, which is a great bet, but that still means that it goes down 27% of the time, and if your retirement is timed incorrectly, running out of money in retirement can be a reality you would not want to face.

History of U.S. Bull & Bear Markets Since 1926

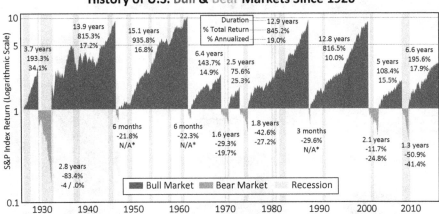

The above graphic illustrates the historical sequence of Bull vs Bear markets. A "Bull" market is defined by one that sustains a 20% or higher gain. A "Bear" market is one that sustains a 20% or higher loss. From this graphic we can see that Bull markets average almost 9 years and Bear markets average just a short 1.4 years, but average 43% loss during that short time period. You can see how dangerous a retirees exposure to these Bear markets can be. Just like you could imagine a bear attack, they are quick and violent and potentially deadly!

The Longevity Challenge

As if the lack of pensions, underfunded Social Security, and market risk weren't enough, there are two other major challenges for today's retirees that have grown to heightened concern: long term care cost and longevity risk.

Years ago, the average American only lived into their late 70's. It was also much more customary to have them live at home with their family and those who chose to hire outside nursing care discovered it was much less expensive than it is today. In fact, the Peter G. Peterson Foundation estimates that health care costs will rise an average of 5.5% per year through 2027. This number is almost four times what overall inflation is and is projected to outpace GDP by 2% each year.

Healthcare spending is projected to grow faster than the economy over the next decade

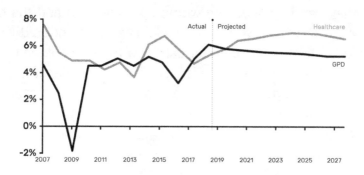

According to a Genworth study, nearly 70% of Americans will need some form of long-term care during their end of life. Not surprisingly, half of that long term care is provided by family, which isn't free! When our family has to provide long term care for us, it ties up their *human capital*, or ability to make money, and those costs can be more than the actual cost of third party administered long-term care. As you probably know, Medicare does not cover the cost for long-term care. With those costs rising faster than any other retirement cost, it's a difficult challenge to conquer.

Worst of all, we are living too long! Yes, it sounds odd, and it's hard to imagine that living longer is a bad thing, but all aforementioned challenges are multiplied the longer you live. For example, if you are retiring and concerned about market risk, and you are expected to live 20% longer than your grandparents lived, then your chances of intersecting a market recession have also increased by 20%. Another example, if inflation is constantly eroding your purchasing power, the longer you live the less purchasing power you will have. The scariest thing of all is that the longer you live, the higher your risk of running out of money!

Could you imagine waking up on your 90th birthday only to find out you have no more money? Sounds crazy, but it is absolutely a possibility considering the numerous challenges that face our retirement.

These challenges are real and they are daunting, but the good news is that they can be conquered with proper planning and the proper tools, which is why I wrote this book. The Fixed Indexed Annuity (FIA) is a relatively new tool that can be a turn-key solution to help prepare a retiree for these challenges. The Seven Benefits of FIAs are at your fingertips, so read on and see how the FIA can benefit your retirement plan.

CHAPTER II

MY STORY

The Early Years

When I was 13 my parents' divorce was finalized and my father moved out for good. As is the norm for kids of divorced parents, they must adjust and take on additional roles. Some are caregivers, some are moral support, and others, like me, help with the finances.

I worked from age 15 on. I started bagging groceries for a regional grocery chain, but when they told me I didn't pay my union dues (I believe they were a mere $100 at the time) I split and went to flip burgers at a local drive in. I spent time parking cars in downtown Seattle and delivered pizza. I found that jobs where you could receive tips were the most lucrative. I even doubled up during a time when I didn't have a college scholarship and worked graveyard at a gas station, which made for some exhausting winter morning workouts.

Yes, I experienced the value of hard work and learned how difficult it can be to get ahead. I certainly felt compassion for all those other Americans who were doing the same thing as me, and I realized how impossible it can seem to envision the future of retiring some day and having enough money saved up so I wouldn't have to work again. For me, just having enough money to buy some new shoes, put gas in my car and go to the movies was a struggle. Yes, I had learned true empathy for the financial struggle that affected millions of Americans.

I was exposed at an early age to the fact that work was more than paying your bills and spending your money. Somewhere between the mortgage, car payment, utility bill, and renting Blockbuster movies, you had to set aside additional money that you would one day live off. Retirement planning was real, and it did not seem easy.

Seeing my mother struggle, despite working full time for the Seattle Archdiocese and receiving support from her ex-husband, was an eye-opener. I realized she, like so many Americans, was going to struggle in retirement and she needed help coming up with a retirement plan.

Education

For both high school and college, scholastic greatness was not my driving force. I was far more interested in the social aspects and my football career than grades. I attended high school at Everett High, north of Seattle, and coasted without much effort to a 3.5 GPA. For college, I originally committed to play tight end at the University of Washington, but a local legend, Jon Kitna (who played 17 seasons as an NFL quarterback), played at a Division II school, Central Washington University, about two hours east of Seattle. So, I thought that attending Central Washington University and playing quarterback behind Jon Kitna would be my path to professional football greatness. In hindsight, neither school was going to lead me to the NFL, due almost entirely to my inability to be as talented as those few who do make it. Consequently, I finished my degree in Business Management with barely a 3.0 GPA and honestly couldn't remember much of what I learned 90 days after I left.

Startups and Entrepreneurship

Shortly after college I took a job and moved down to San Francisco. I was there at the peak time of the "dot-com" boom. I was even involved in a new dot-com startup. At the tender age of 23, I knew nothing about starting, running, or selling a company but was still considered a co-founder of our fledgling corporation, which we ended up selling (through no real contribution of mine) for multiple seven figures.

After having such early success, I was programmed that a traditional 40-hour a week job was *not* the path to success. This is quite unfortunate, because I didn't realize how much luck was involved in my early career, and I was now looking for a shortcut to my next big payoff.

As all "too good to be true" stories do, the dot-com story ended abruptly, and the market plummeted in 2001. By this time, I had left the Bay Area and moved back to Seattle, where I bounced around from one startup to another, hoping to recapture the success that was achieved just a few short years earlier. The reality was that I was lost, any money I made in our startup venture was long gone, and I had no direction as to where I should go or what I should do next.

Reality Strikes

By 2005 I had started to realize that at age 30, I had not saved up any retirement of my own. Although I had been involved in decent-paying roles with various startups and even had one company sell, I had spent the money I made in between startups and on funding the failed startups and was looking at starting from $0 when it came to my retirement. This is when I realized I needed to refocus on a career that provided a more stable opportunity for growth within my skill set.

I very deliberately analyzed the successful people I knew. I examined what they were doing and what made them successful. I did not have a Stanford MBA or attended Wharton School of Business. I wasn't a member of the Black Skulls, and I didn't come from money. So, what would I do?

I reflected on the successful people I went to school with and evaluated what they were doing and what I perceived their competencies were. I was looking for people who had similar skill sets as mine. All signs pointed to the insurance and finance profession, so that is where I reinvented myself.

When I started, I focused on life, home, auto and health insurance. Financial planning was the last thing on my mind. I believed that my background and close relationship with startup and technology companies would give me an advantage with these "commodity-based" sales.

After one year of managing this multi-line approach to insurance, I realized that most of the revenue came from life insurance sales, and something called an annuity, so I sold off the other insurance lines and focused on life insurance and annuities. This was the foundation of retirement planning for me.

Retirement Planning Begins

In 2009, I sold the home, auto and health insurance portions of the business. This allowed me to focus solely on life insurance and annuity sales. I learned that most life insurance and annuities are purchased to compliment some sort of financial plan. At that point, I felt a surge of desire to learn everything I could about investing and wealth management. Now, "investing and wealth management" is a very broad field. Similar to how doctors specialize in one aspect of medicine or surgery, financial planning is often best when an advisor or firm specializes in a specific field of focus. I chose to focus on helping people who were in retirement or preparing for retirement, a field that is generally known as "retirement planning." This desire was forged during my days growing up and helping my single mom with her finances and knowing how much fulfillment I found helping her and other people in her situation.

I enjoyed learning all about peoples' retirement options. I have always felt that when I helped someone learn how to best *save* for retirement and also how to best *spend* their retirement, I knew I was doing something that would truly and absolutely have a positive impact on their lives. Later, I worked to obtain my securities license but wasn't as interested in making the sales of stocks and bonds my focus, so I switched to an emphasis on estate planning, which is where I gained my first designation of Certified Estate Planner (CEP). After gaining momentum and experience working with attorneys, CPAs, and financial advisors while helping clients with their estate planning, I wanted to launch deeper into retirement planning. When the American College of Finance launched their Retirement Income Certified Professional (RICP®) designation, I jumped on the opportunity. To this day, I believe it was the most valuable and applicable certification I've ever gained.

I most recently completed the Wealth Management Certified Professional (WMCP®) designation from the American College of Finance, and I am also an Investment Advisor Representative at my own firm, Ruggiero Wealth Management. I've rounded this out with a National Social Security Advisor (NSSA) certificate, because Social Security planning is such a vital part of Middle-America's retirement (more about that in a later section).

Please understand, I am not boasting about the certifications I have. It is important for the reader to know my education because it explains that I am not just an annuity representative trying to sell annuities. I am a fiduciary (I do what is in the client's best interest) who believes in Fixed Indexed Annuities!

During my career, I have been able to help hundreds of clients across the Northwest, including retirees from Microsoft, Boeing, and Amazon to name a few. I was also able to teach other agents who needed guidance on how to advise their clients and what products and plans would be best for every unique situation. This responsibility was something I thoroughly enjoyed, and it drove me to learn even more about retirement planning, which is a true passion for me today and will continue to drive me in the future.

I often think about how much time I wasted in school not working to my ability when it came to my studies. I realized later that I was simply focused on football at the time, not school. Once football was over, retirement planning became my passion, and I attacked it with every bit of fervor and dedication as I did during my years playing football.

As of 2020 I had personally helped clients with more than $50,000,000 of retirement income planning. This number is more impactful when you consider that I worked almost exclusively with the underserved "Middle Americans." Those folks who had a couple hundred thousand dollars of retirement assets, not millions of dollars.

I was a corporate advisor for a nationwide financial marketing organization, where I developed and trained over 12,000 licensed agents and advisors to nearly $600,000,000 in six short years. As an advocate for indexing awareness, I started Safe Money Smart (www.safemoneysmart.org), which is a nonprofit entity dedicated to the exploration and education of risk-free and reduced cost planning in retirement along with sound financial structure.

I haven't ignored my passion for startups and technology. In 2015, I founded Xeddi Software and launched InsuranceDrip (InsuranceDrip.com). InsuranceDrip is the first and only turn-key, fully automated multi-digital marketing platform built specifically for insurance financial professionals. InsuranceDrip was presented in the 2016 Digital Insurance Agenda awards in Barcelona and was voted one of the top 100 InsurTech startups from 2015-2018.

In 2018 I launched AnnuityHub (annuityhub.com), which is the fastest way for the public to find the best fixed indexed annuity for their retirement needs online.

Most recently, in 2020, my company was purchased by the largest distributor of senior benefit products in the World. I proudly serve as a Managing Partner with that entity as I finish writing this book for you.

I wrote this book to help two people: those who need help with their retirement planning (consumers) and those who are looking to help others with their retirement planning (agents and advisors). The motivation was simple. I believe that the use of stocks and bonds in retirement is overdone and results in far too much risk and far too little security, guarantees, and predictability for retirees. I also believe that too many retirees lose large sums of money to hidden fees, which can erode their retirement nest-egg. Most importantly, retirees need to have a legitimate and affordable tool for removing risk and fees, while offering the potential for lifetime income, long term care alternatives and legacy planning. The fixed indexed annuity is a fantastic, turn-key tool that can deliver those solutions for millions of Americans today and in the future.

CHAPTER III

TRADITIONAL RETIREMENT

Just as humans have a life cycle where we are born, mature, decline, and eventually pass, our finances also have a lifecycle. Not surprisingly, this is called our *financial life cycle*, and understanding it is an important part of proper retirement planning.

Three Phases of the Financial Life Cycle

There are numerous variations of the financial life cycle, but I prefer the simplest three-phase version, accumulation, protection, decumulation.

The first phase of our financial life cycle is *accumulation*. Early in our lives, our most valuable asset is our *human capital*, which is the time and energy we have and can dedicate toward earning money and accumulating *financial capital*. Protecting human capital is the reason we purchase life insurance, and in my opinion, is the reason why everyone should have a life insurance policy during their accumulation years. When we think of someone in their 20s or 30s, we think of someone who hasn't yet accumulated much financial capital, but they are learning, gaining experience, and getting raises (whether they work as an employee or self-employed). They are essentially "trading" their human capital for financial capital with the hopes that they will complete their primary accumulation phase (age 60+) with enough assets to finish out their career and retire comfortably.

The second phase is *asset protection* (also known as retirement readiness). This phase is where we have accumulated the majority of our financial capital and the additional contributions we make to our retirement nest-egg are not as important as protecting (and growing) our retirement nest-egg. It is at this phase where Fixed Indexed Annuities (FIAs) enter the picture.

The last phase is *decumulation*. The decumulation phase is where we *spend* our financial capital. It is a very delicate phase and is highly dependent on the first two phases. Many professionals will argue the importance of a 4th phase (*end of life spending/health care costs*), and 5th phase (*legacy planning*), but for this book, I prefer to keep it simple.

With legacy planning, almost all my clients have had a desire to leave something to their loved ones, but we have enough challenges facing us to get to the finish line, so let's focus on the three phases in this book, and if there is anything left over for the kids and grandkids, that is a bonus! Now, let's take a more detailed look at the three phases of our financial life cycle.

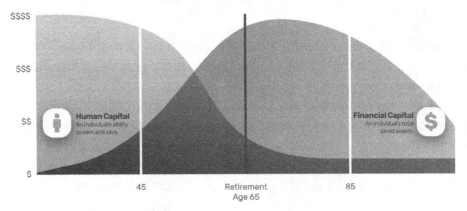

Three Phases Of Financial Lifecycle Exchanging Human Capital for Financial Capital

Phase One – Accumulation

Since the inception of the 401k in 1980, retirement has shifted to be centered around stocks, bonds, and mutual funds. The basic concept being that a retiree during their accumulation years (20-50+) can invest with regular intervals and take advantage of something called *Dollar Cost Averaging* (DCA). DCA results in an average price paid that is less than the average cost of the stock or fund. In fact, it can be beneficial for the market to be down during someone's accumulation years! Sound odd? Look at this example.

If you are investing $500 a month toward your retirement, and the mutual fund you are investing in has dropped from $25/share to $20/share, then your $500 monthly investment will now gain you 5 additional shares (20 to 25) so you now own more shares of the fund. Assuming the fund will eventually go back up, you now have increased wealth due to the early decline in the stock price.

I consider DCA investments into the stock market to still be the best way to accumulate wealth for retirement, and with the

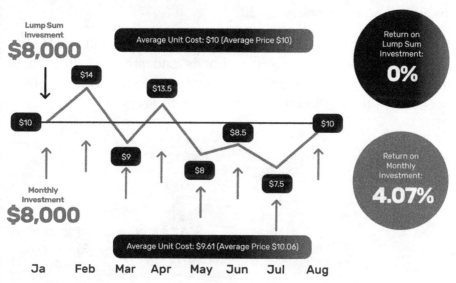

Dollar Cost Averaging (DCA) In Action

competitive landscape of so many money managers wanting to facilitate a company's defined contribution plan (like 401k's) the fees tend to be very low, which is a benefit to retirees during their accumulation years. Look at the graphic on the previous page and see how DCA works to benefit you.

Phase Two — Asset Protection

Many retirement plans fail before retirement even begins. This neglected period starts approximately 5-7 years *before* retirement. At this point, the retiree has accumulated the bulk of their wealth, and they need to start shifting from the *accumulation* phase to *asset protection* phase. Unfortunately, the lack of tools and education (and very little incentive for many of the financial advisors who manage these funds to use those tools) have left many retirees unprepared for the final phase of their financial lives. These pre-retirees are left in higher risk investments that can drop the value of their nest-egg dramatically overnight. We saw this in 2000-2002, 2008, and again in March of 2020.

The move from more risky equities (stocks/mutual funds/ETFs) to less risky investments, such as bonds and preferred stock prior to retirement is known as a *Glidepath*. Glidepath can be critical because, in theory, it limits the exposure to declines.

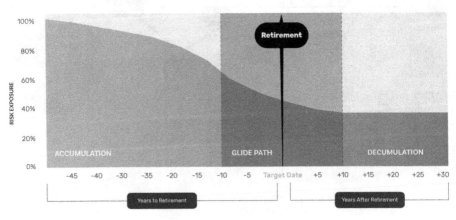

For example, if Mr. Smith is 57 years old and plans on retiring at age 65 and he has accumulated $500,000. What does he hope to gain over the next seven years and what can he afford to lose? For most retirees, the thought of "taking a step backwards" is far too scary to try and earn an extra 5–10% on their portfolio. By moving these investments to more conservative alternatives, the risk of loss is reduced, and the attention is focused on preparing for retirement.

It is also important to remember how much is needed to gain back any losses in the market. If Mr. Smith lost 20% of his nest-egg ($100,000) he would be left with $400,000. If he gains 20% back the next year, he would only be gaining back $80,000, not the $100,000 he lost. In fact, he would have to gain back 25% to get back to the original $500,000 he had before the market drop. The graphic below shows the relationship between losses and recovery gains when we look at a percentage.

What Would It Take To Earn Back Your Losses?

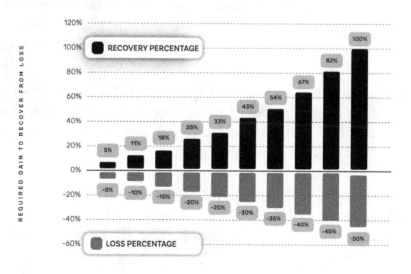

I always ask my clients three questions to assess if they are ready for the protection phase of their financial life cycles:

1. How much more are you hoping to gain?
2. How much of your retirement are you willing to lose?
3. What do you want your retirement to do for you?

These are very straightforward and simple questions, but I am continually amazed when I ask them and the client can't answer them. Typically, the answers are "well, I don't really want to lose anything." and "I don't know how much more I am hoping to gain." and "I guess I'll use the money to retire on."

My point is that they have no plan. If you can't answer these questions specifically, then you don't have a plan!

For most Americans, they do not want to lose any more money once they hit age 50+. They are intolerant of loss and if losses do happen, it can be an extremely stressful occurrence for them to endure. They also tend to have no accumulation goal in mind. I have rarely met a client who professes, "I currently have $300,000 saved up and I'll retire when I hit $330,000!" Why is that? Here are the two reasons:

1. While accumulating this money, they are disconnected from the money they put away for retirement. The money isn't even seen on their paycheck and they know they aren't going to touch it until later in the future.

2. They have no control of the market! For most Americans, their planning stopped when they decided how much of their paycheck they were going to put into their 401k. Everything after that they are flying blind.

The last question (What do you want your retirement to do for you?) is where retirement planning really starts. In fact, you can argue that the first two questions can't be answered until the third question is. For example, I had a client that told me they "didn't really want to lose anything" and "they would like to make a little bit more" and "they would like to take $1,000 a month from their retirement at age 62 when they retired to live off of." In this scenario, we determined that they had saved enough already to satisfy the goal. If they kept the money exposed to market risk (they were almost 100% in equities) and they gained 10% more, it would not yield them a significant amount more of monthly retirement income, but if they lost 10%, they would fall short of the $1,000 a month retirement income goal. In this example we see how someone was ready to retire and didn't know it. Further exposure to the market could only jeopardize their retirement.

If you have saved up $500,000 for retirement and you lose *just* 5% ($25,000) ask yourself, *"how long did it take me to save up that $25,000 I just lost? How long could I have lived off that $25,000 I just lost? What could I have purchased with that $25,000 I just lost?"* For most, the answers regarding these questions of loss are terrifying, so it is important to protect what you have first, and all other planning is subsequent.

Phase two, Asset Protection, or Glidepath, is not only the phase where we protect our funds, but also the phase where we start to create a plan for our spending and decumulation. I do think it is important to note, that in some instances, having some clients' funds continually exposed to equities for long-term growth and fighting inflation is an integral part of the retirement plan, but not when it comes to risking the foundation of the clients' base income and fundamental retirement goals.

Phase Three – Decumulation

When we think of retirement, we think of the third phase; decumulation, which is where we spend the money we have saved up. It has often been said, retirement is like a permanent weekend, no work and all play. Since weekends are when we spend most of our money on a per diem basis, it is critically important to have a plan.

I have always subscribed to the concept of having two pools of spending money. The first pool is for your *necessity* spending, like mortgage payment, car insurance, food, utilities, etc. The second pool is for your *discretionary* spending, like eating out, going to the movies, or travel. One of the best retirement planning teachers of all time, Tom Hegna, uses the term *"Paychecks & Playchecks"* to describe the two different pools of spending (Tom's book Paychecks & Playchecks can be purchased on Amazon or at TomHegna.com). This is where a Fixed Indexed Annuity offering guaranteed lifetime income, or "paychecks," is hugely valuable to make sure that your necessity spending is taken care of. Let's face it, you might have to wait for airfare to drop in price before you book that trip to Paris, but it wouldn't stress you out like waiting for the stock market to rise in order for you to make your mortgage payment or pay your doctor's bill!

Calculating your necessity spending from your discretionary spending can be done in many ways, but I've created a *Retirement Income QuickSheet* that you can use. It is important to also take this time to document what type of income you have and how much to expect. This is where you can see if you have a deficit or a surplus, and it can help you decide how much guaranteed income you would need from an FIA (or other income annuity). Keep in mind, having a surplus does not mean you should forgo an FIA. In fact, having a surplus could mean that you should fervently look to protect and grow that surplus (which is a trademark of the FIA) so you don't end up having a deficit later on in retirement.

Retirement Income QuickSheet

INCOME			
FIXED		**VARIABLE**	
SSI primary		Business	
SSI spouse		RMDs	
Pensions		Stocks/Bonds	
Disability		Inheritance	
Annuities		Other	
Other			
TOTAL		TOTAL	

EXPENSES			
FIXED		**VARIABLE**	
Mortgage/Rent		Travel	
Housing Costs		Hobby	
Food/Clothing		Recreation	
Vehicles		Gifts	
Medical		Charity	
Other		Other	
TOTAL		TOTAL	

TOTAL			
FIXED		**VARIABLE**	
Income		Income	
- Expenses		- Expenses	
TOTAL +/-		TOTAL +/-	

Your IRA

For most Americans, their largest retirement savings is going to be some form of a *defined contribution plan*. Defined contribution plans first appeared as the 401k in 1980. Since then the pension has become almost obsolete and the defined contribution plan has been the most common form of retirement savings. These plans include 401k, 403b, 457, TSP, SEP, and other plans regulated by the IRS. Regardless of the plan type, once we are done contributing to the plan and we shift toward retirement, these funds are allocated into an Individual Retirement Account, or IRA.

These plans collectively are called "qualified" plans. That means that they qualify for rules the IRS has set forth. Some of the basic rules are listed below:

1. These contributions can be pre-tax (reducing your income at time of investment, and taxed as income at time of withdrawal)

2. There is a 10% "penalty" tax if you withdraw the funds prior to age 59.5 (there are some exceptions, like education, disability, first-time home purchases, and Rule 72t)

3. You are required to take out a certain & increasing percentage of your qualified account starting at age 72. This is called your Required Minimum Distribution (RMD)

Participating in a defined contribution plan, when possible, is key because it is the most common way for Americans to save any sort of significant amount of savings for retirement.

We tend to live paycheck to paycheck, and when we do get ahead with our cash savings, we get a surprise expenditure, such as a broken transmission in our car, a new hospital bill, an unexpected veterinarian visit, or the dozens of other costs that tend to pop up out of nowhere. Because defined contribution plans are funded with money taken out of our paycheck before we get paid, then it is essentially money we never see. So, they can accumulate without being disrupted by life's daily struggles.

Therefore, understanding where our retirement is going to come from and how to protect and grow it is key. Here are three suggestions that should keep you on the right track for retirement.

1. Always invest up to the employer match if you can. There is nothing better than free money. For example, if an employer is going to match your contributions up to 4%, then you need to scratch and claw to at least hit that 4%!

2. Be more aggressive in your allocations during your accumulation years. There are laws that require employers to give you multiple options to invest in for your defined contribution plan. While you are accumulating wealth, I encourage you to consider choosing the more aggressive options (selecting more equities over bonds) and remember, as crazy as it sounds, having a few down markets during your accumulation years can benefit you!

3. Remember the glidepath! It is important to start shifting your allocations of your defined contribution plan toward safer and more conservative investments as early as seven years before you retire.

By following these three guidelines, and properly planning your Social Security income, you should be on your way to a happy and enjoyable retirement!

CHAPTER IV

WHAT THE HECK IS AN FIA?

The DNA of the FIA

The Fixed Indexed Annuity, or FIA was first introduced in 1995 by a company called Keyport Life. So, in financial evolutionary terms, the FIA is relatively new. According to Wink's Sales & Market Report, FIAs made up nearly 27% of all deferred annuity sales (please visit www.winkintel.com for the most comprehensive and accurate annuity industry data, and thank you Sheryl). Why is that?

If I were going to give a sales pitch for FIAs in a few short words, I would say, "FIAs allow you to *participate* in upside gains in the market, lock those gains in when achieved, never participate in the downside market loss, and have the ability to create a paycheck for life."

Sound too good to be true? The key is understanding that the FIA *participates* in the market gains, but it does not capture *all* the market gains or *beat* the market gains. You must understand what the FIA is, how it works, and most importantly what to expect from it before you consider purchasing one for your retirement.

I am going to explain what a *Fixed Indexed Annuity* is by first explaining what a *Fixed Annuity* is. A fixed annuity, also called a *multi-year guaranteed annuity* or MYGA, is the simplest form of an accumulation annuity, that is, an annuity not specifically designed for lifetime income, but rather for safe accumulation of interest. A fixed annuity is a relatively short-term annuity, say three, five, or seven years. It guarantees you a fixed amount of interest to be credited to your principal, normally on an annual basis. The longer the term, the higher the interest credit (this is not necessarily true in very rare instances of flat or inverted yield curves). This is because the longer the term, the longer investments the annuity company can purchase (primarily investment grade bonds) and get a higher yield, which they share with you. For example, if you were looking at a three-year fixed annuity, it might offer a 2% yield, but a seven-year could offer 4%.

A Fixed Indexed Annuity works very similar to a Fixed Annuity. The difference lies in what the annuity company does with your yield. Rather than guaranteeing you a fixed 2% or 3% or 4% annual return (like the MYGA does), the FIA guarantees you a 0% return and use all your yield to purchase something called a *call option*.

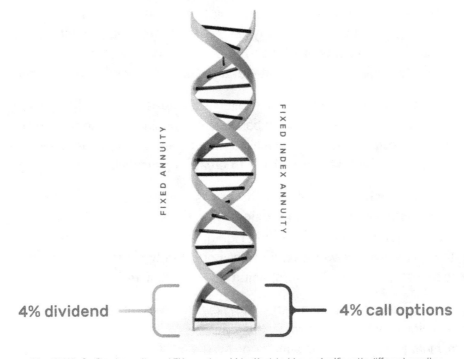

FIXED ANNUITY

FIXED INDEX ANNUITY

4% dividend — 4% call options

The "DNA" of a Fixed annuity and FIA are almost identical, but have significantly different results

The Call Option

Option trading can be complex once you dig into the many types of options that can be purchased and sold, but a call option is very easy to understand. With a call option, you are buying the rights to purchase something at a later fixed date. Let me explain how a call option works with an analogous example.

Let's say you had your eye on a house for sale. You saw that it was going on the market for $150,000 and you asked the owner, "If I give you $1,000 today, can I reserve the right to buy your house for $150,000 next year?" The owner says yes, and you now have the right to buy the house for $150,000 for the next 365 days. One of two things will happen. Either the house will go up in value, maybe to $175,000, and you can then buy it for $150,000 and immediately sell it for $175,000 and profit $24,000 ($175,000 − $150,000 − $1,000 for the cost of the option). On the other hand, the house might not get much demand, or the market might get soft and the house goes down in value to $140,000. In this instance, you would never exercise your right to buy it at the higher price of $150,000 so you let your "option" expire, and you are only out the $1,000 for the price of the option.

Annuity companies do this exact same thing with your interest yield on your principal inside the FIA. Rather than just giving you a fixed return (let's say 3%), they take that 3% and purchase call options on an index. If that index rises over the next year (remember, an index will track the market), then you get the payoff on the anniversary of the option purchase. If the index declines, your options expire, and you gain zero for that year.

So why is this better than a fixed annuity? Well, if you isolate any one year, the FIA could be worse than a fixed annuity because if the market goes down, the FIA will earn 0% and the MYGA will return 3%. However, the historical data shows that the FIA, which is driven indirectly by market growth, will outpace the fixed annuity return over time. Or, at least it has the *potential* for higher returns.

Think of the call option as a "force multiplier." It allows a 3% return-on-investment to become a 5%, 8%, 11%, or even 20% return. Now, please understand, expecting 20% on an FIA is foolhardy, because it rarely happens, but it *has* happened, and it is that higher potential payout that makes them attractive. Even if the FIA only average 3.5% or 4% over the course of ten years, that will still outpace a fixed annuity offering a guaranteed 3%.

For example, one of my favorite annuity companies (which will remain nameless here) has numerous indexing options that have achieved double-digit returns for their clients in certain years. I know this because I have written them for my clients, and I have seen the statements. Look at the redacted statement shown here. Again, this is not typical, but with this kind of potential upside combined with protection from market loss, many clients are rightfully attracted to the appeal of an FIA.

Your Interest Crediting Strategies Summarized

Strategies	Starting Strategy Value	Strategy Interest Credited	Total Withdrawals	Ending Strategy Value
Fixed	$0.00	$0.00	$0.00	$0.00
1-Yr Point-to-Point ▄▄▄	$0.00	$0.00	$0.00	$0.00
1-Yr Monthly Cap ▄▄▄	$0.00	$0.00	$0.00	$0.00
2-Yr Point-to-Point ▄▄▄▄▄	$121,051.83	$49,048.00	$1,259.57	$168,840.26
1-Yr Point-to-Point ▄▄▄▄	$128,854.11	$21,658.29	$1,114.53	$149,397.87
Total	$249,905.94	$70,706.29	$2,374.10	$318,238.13

How Your Interest Credit This Year

Data is displayed for strategies with a term end date of 1/22/2018 and a starting or ending strategy value greater than $0.

Strategies	Rate Type	Current Rate	Strategy Index % Change	Rate of Interest Credited	End of Term Interest Credited
2-Yr Point-to-Point ▄▄▄	Participation Rate Annual Spread	100.00% 0.75%	42.01%	40.52%	$49,048.00
1-Yr Point-to-Point ▄▄▄	Participation Rate	65.00%	25.85%	16.81%	$21,658.29

What Is an Index?

It is important to understand that an FIA is not directly investing in stocks or the market. It is not purchasing mutual funds or ETFs. It is purchasing call options on an index (thus, the "indexed" in fixed *indexed* annuities). So, we have reviewed what call options are, but what is an index?

An index is a measurement of something. When it comes to finance, an index is a measurement of change in a securities market. It would be too difficult to track every single security that trades in the United States, and some of them frankly are not worth tracking (meaning they don't have enough market capitalization to give us any insight into the economy), so we take a sample of securities as a representative of the whole—similar to the way pollsters use surveys to gauge the sentiment of the population. The measurement of that smaller sample is called an index.

There are many popular indexes. Some you might have heard of, like the Dow Jones or the S&P 500, and others you might not have, like the Russell 2000. Here are some of the most common indexes in existence:

> **S&P 500:** The S&P 500 index is a basket of 500 of the largest U.S. stocks weighted by market capitalization, or how much revenue they bring in. The index is widely considered to be the best indicator of how large U.S. stocks are performing on a day-to-day basis. The top five largest weighted companies in 2016 were Apple (AAPL), Microsoft (MSFT), Exxon Mobil (XOM), Johnson & Johnson (JNJ), and General Electric (GE). Just two years later, the S&P top five were Apple (AAPL), Microsoft (MSFT), Amazon (AMZN), Google (GOOG), and Facebook (FB). This shows you how the index is fluid, or "free-floating," and its movement follows the markets closely.

Dow Jones: The Dow Jones Industrial Average is a price-weighted average of thirty significant stocks traded on the New York Stock Exchange and the NASDAQ. The Dow Jones was invented by Charles Dow in 1896. When the TV networks say, "the market is up today," they are generally referring to the Dow. Unlike the S&P 500, which agnostically ranks their 500 companies by revenue, the Dow Jones has their thirty contributing companies chosen through an administrative review.

NASDAQ: Like both the S&P 500 and the Dow Jones, the NASDAQ is an index that tracks certain companies based on their capitalization. However, it tracks 4,000 companies, which is considered a more comprehensive sample of the overall markets.

The above indexes are often used with FIAs. As an example, if you purchased a $100,000 FIA on January 20, 2017 that is indexed with the S&P 500, that means it buys one year call options on the S&P 500 (there are also two-year call options). On the purchase date (January 20th, 2017), the S&P 500 was at 2,271. One year later, on January 20th, 2018, when the call option was going to expire, the S&P 500 was at 2,798, which represents a gain of 527 points, or 23.2%. Obviously, your call options would be exercised, and your account would be credited.

How much will your account be credited? Remember, FIAs allow you to *participate* in the market gains, not exceed them or take all of them. So, you will get some of the gains, and how much of the gains depends on the issuer of the FIA and the indexing strategy you chose.

It is important to note that the annuity company must cover costs for the administrative purchase of the options, along with creating certain "hedges" on the call investments. They credit your account using the movement of the index and filter it with either a spread, cap, or participation rate.

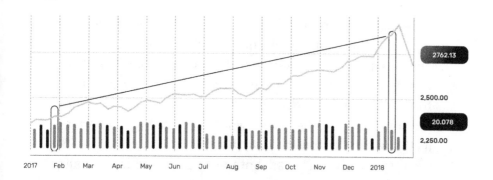

2762.13

2,500.00

20.078

2,250.00

2017 Feb Mar Apr May Jun Jul Aug Sep Oct Nov Dec 2018

This above graphic shows the S&P 500 from January 20th, 2017 to January 20th, 2018, a 23% climb

Caps, Spreads, and Participation Rates

There are three types of filters that annuity companies use to determine the actual crediting to your account based on the index's performance. These are caps, spreads, and participation rates. Let's dive into these for a better understanding:

> **Caps:** A cap was the first form of crediting that an FIA used and is still in use today. A cap is very easy to understand because it "caps" the returns that can be credited to your account. Caps can change based on market climate, but they will always stay competitive so the annuity companies can earn new business. An example would be a 5% cap. If the index returned 7%, the client would be credited 5%. The benefit to this is that you get all crediting for an index that is below the cap, meaning if the index only returned 3%, you would get 100% of 3%, which has value. The downside is that you will not get higher returns in banner years for the index, such as the S&P 500 in 2017. Although caps were the first crediting method used, they are largely being phased out in favor of participation rates.

Spreads: A spread works by having a percentage, or "spread," that comes off first to the annuity company and then the rest goes to the client. Think of it as the opposite of a cap. For example, let's say a spread for an FIA on the S&P 500 index was 2%. If the index returns 3%, then the client would only get 1%; however, if the index returned 14%, the client would get 12% interest credited. The advantage to a spread is opposite that of a cap. In a year when the index returns a lower amount (1% to 5%), the spread will be unfavorable, but in banner years (6%+), the spread allows for higher returns. Spreads, like caps, are being phased out by participation rates.

Participation Rates: The newest and most popular form of interest crediting for FIAs is called participation rates. A participation rate determines how much, or what percentage, of an index's returns will be credited to a client's FIA. For example, if you had an FIA that had a 60% participation rate on the S&P 500 index, and the index went up 20%, your FIA would be credited 60% of the 20%, or 12%. Participation rates are widely viewed as the fairest form of interest crediting, and that is why they are growing in popularity and replacing caps and spreads in many instances.

The following graphic is a visual representation of the difference between caps, spreads, and participation rates. In each index crediting strategy, the index (let's say the NASDAQ) for one year returned 12%. Let's also assume this FIA has a 4% cap, a 4% spread, and a 70% participation rate. You can see how each crediting strategy would have performed.

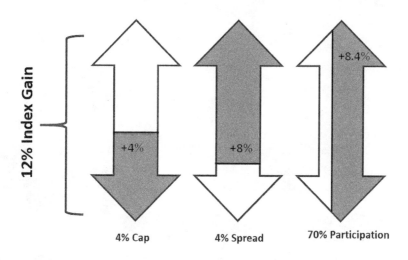

Now, look at the hypothetical performance of each when the index returned 3%

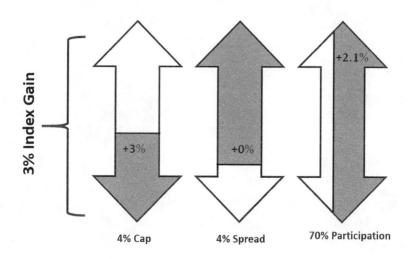

Now that we have reviewed what an FIA is and how it works, let's look at how it can benefit your retirement plan. This is where we discover the Seven Benefits of FIAs for Retirement!

CHAPTER V

SEVEN BENEFITS OF FIAS FOR RETIREMENT

Welcome to the *Seven Benefits of Fixed Indexed Annuities*. These seven powerful benefits are found in every FIA. Now that you know more about your retirement and what an FIA is, you are ready to explore these seven benefits.

Benefit One – The Power of Indexing

What would a fixed indexed annuity be without indexing? Well, it would be a fixed annuity, as explained earlier. I also discussed what indexing is and how it works. So *why* is indexing so powerful? Let me explain.

As we learned, the markets are a great place to build wealth and accumulate retirement, but as we get closer toward our retirement goal, we need to choose ways of protecting that wealth (remember glide path?). Ideally, we would like to find this protection without giving up the ability to make decent gains when the market *does* go up, and not have to worry about when to buy and when to sell. That, in a nutshell, is what indexing accomplishes. Let's break that down further.

The protection of indexing comes from our guarantee to never lose money when the market is down. There is a saying in our industry that "zero is the hero." What is meant by this is that your guarantee in an FIA is 0%, but when the market drops, like it did in 2001, 2008, and 2020, having a 0% guarantee can be a lifesaver. If the market lost 15% and you lost 0%, wouldn't that essentially be a 15% gain? *That* is why "zero is the hero."

The second part of indexing that is less talked about, but every bit as powerful as zero market losses, is called *locked in gains*. Every year that your FIA goes up, those gains are "locked in." This means that your new guaranteed minimum account value is your original principle, plus any gains from that year and all previous years. So, unlike investments directly into the stock market where a "bear market" can erase several years of gains, the FIA always keeps any gains it achieves. That is the power of indexing.

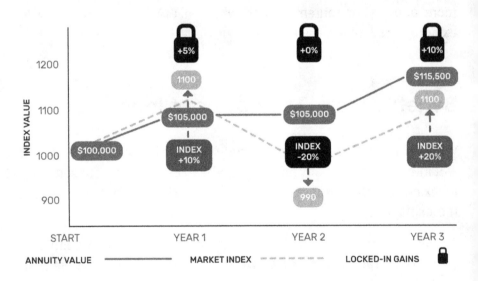

This becomes especially powerful in periods of market volatility. As you can see in the hypothetical example above, if the market goes up 10% year one, your FIA participates in those gains (say 5%), but then the following year the market goes down 20%, your funds are locked in at the high-water mark from the year before. Better still, when the market does rebound (as is the norm after a market decline), then your FIA participates in those gains too, but from a higher trajectory because it never participated in the losses!

We've all heard the saying "buy low and sell high." The power of indexing essentially allows you to do this on an automated level. When the market is down, you are essentially "buying in," and when the market rises, you are essentially "selling high." There is always an aspect of timing and a bit of luck involved to maximize those returns, but it's far superior to risking market losses and having to "guess" when to buy and when to sell.

There was a study done in 2015 that shows a very compelling statistic. As you can see from the graphic below, even though the market (S&P 500) returned an average of 8.2% each year from 1996–2015 (this number is considered "Total Return" and includes dividends), the average investor only returned 2.1% during that same time. This is due to human psychology and our reality that most of us are savers, not investors.

20-Year Annualized Returns by Asset Class (1996-2015)

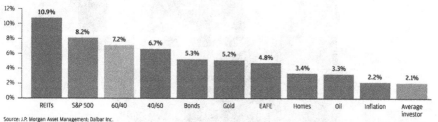

Source: J.P. Morgan Asset Management; Dalbar Inc.

Indexes used are as follows: REITs: NAREIT Equity REIT Index; EAFE: MSCI EAFE; Oil: WTI Index; Bonds: Barclays U.S. Aggregate Index; Homes: median sale price of existing single-family homes; Gold: USD/troy oz; Inflation: CPI; 60/40: A balanced portfolio with 60% invested in S&P 500 Index and 40% invested in high-quality U.S. fixed income, represented by the Barclays U.S. Aggregate Index. The portfolio is rebalanced annually. Average asset allocation investor return is based on an analysis by Dalbar Inc., which utilizes the net of aggregate mutual fund sales, redemptions and exchanges each month as a measure of investor behavior. Returns are annualized (and total return where applicable) and represent the 20-year period ending 12/31/15 to match Dalbar's most recent analysis.
Source: "Guide to the Markets" – U.S. data are as of December 31, 2016

This leads me to another benefit of indexing that is seldom talked about, but in my experience one of the most powerful benefits of indexing. That is the benefit of eliminating emotion!

Unfortunately, people tend to do the opposite of what is ideal (remember, we are largely savers, not investors). When the market is climbing, we tend to not want to sell because we get greedy and we are afraid of missing out on more gains. Conversely, when the market starts to slide, we panic and sell too early. These are emotional reactions, and they are completely avoided when your funds are in an FIA.

This phenomenon is best told with the story of the elephant and the rider. In this analog, we know that the elephant represents our emotion, and the rider (or driver) is our rationale. The best of plans is controlled by our rational side, but when outside factors, such as fear, anger, stress, etc. come into play, the emotion, or elephant, can take control. Which of these two is stronger, the elephant or the rider? Obviously, it is the elephant, which for most of us is a true depiction of how our emotions can take over in challenging times.

Who is in control when your retirement needs it most?

These emotional reactions are built into our DNA through our subconscious, which is designed to keep us out of danger. However, when emotion affects our financial decisions, it is usually causing us to do the *wrong* thing in times of financial distress.

The fixed indexed annuity works on "auto-pilot" so the emotion of when to buy and when to sell never comes into play, and since the FIA never participates in market losses, we will never find ourselves facing that fear and subsequently reacting to it while in retirement. If you ask me, that alone is worth some serious consideration for your retirement plan!

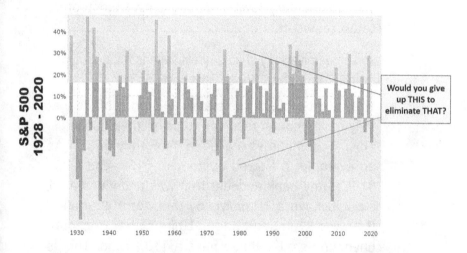

Have you ever known a financial instrument that could gain double digits during bull markets and lose nothing in bear markets? The FIA has that potential.

Benefit Two – Securities and Guarantees

Keeping retirement funds safe is a dominant concern of most retirees. Safety can be in the form of protecting against market loss, or it can be in the form of protecting against financial default of the institution that holds your retirement funds. The fixed indexed annuity provides both forms of safety.

Legal Reserve Status: Annuities are not federally regulated. They are regulated at the state level. For most people, this is preferred, and I would agree. It is much more difficult to oversee fifty states and create and enforce laws and regulations to benefit all fifty states' residents than it is for a single state to oversee and regulate what is best for their residents.

Each state has a Department of Insurance (or equivalent) and a commissioner who is elected to run that department. Collectively, they will determine what insurance and annuity laws will best serve and protect their state's residents.

There are some universally shared qualifications for a company to do business in a state. Those qualifications are:

1. They must prove to the state's insurance office that they have enough reserves to cover their liabilities. This is sometimes called a "solvency ratio." As an example, if I owed customers $100, and I had $100 in my bank account that was unencumbered, I would have a 1:1 solvency ratio (or 100% ratio). If I owed $100 and I had $110 in my bank account unencumbered, I would have a 110% ratio. This is essentially the same thing that is required by the states for the annuity companies who wish to sell annuities in their state. The minimum solvency ratio required is 100%.

2. All annuity companies must prove to the state's insurance office that they have most of their portfolio invested in *investment grade* (meaning BBB or higher rated) securities. These low-risk investments are almost exclusively in the form of bonds, which annuity companies purchase directly from the offering institutions at a discount. This

rule goes back to the 1980s (which predates many of these regulations that have now been formed) when annuity companies were seeking riskier and riskier investments to gain an edge over their opponents and create more yield for their customers. The result was that a few entities ended up becoming over-leveraged, could no longer keep their financial promises, and risked default. That was the genesis of the safeguard rules that we have today, and the reason why state insurance offices won't allow for high-risk investments for an annuity company doing business in their state.

3. All annuity companies must pay into a guarantee fund (similar to how banks pay into the FDIC fund). This fund will cover consumers if an annuity or insurance company goes into receivership. Each state offers different limits. Some are higher, like Washington State ($500,000 at time of this writing), and some are lower (usually no lower than $250,000). It is important to know that, although this fund exists, it is strictly prohibited for a sales agent to use this "guarantee" as a way of marketing an annuity or life insurance sale.

4. Annuity and insurance companies will purchase certain levels of re-insurance. Re-insurance is exactly what it sounds like. It is insurance against default. For annuity and insurance companies to maintain desirable levels of liability to assets ratios, they will purchase re-insurance. This is another level of guarantees offered with an FIA.

Collectively, these three qualifiers determine if an annuity company can do business in your state. If they meet these qualifications, then they are considered a legal reserve entity and they can solicit their products in your state.

Financial Rating Companies: One constant I have seen in my years of working with consumers on their financial planning is their amazing desire to seek inputs and guidance from those who are not qualified to provide it! I have seen it all: uncles who opened an online trading account and now consider themselves the next Warren Buffet; sisters who say "I wouldn't do that" to every investment concept under the sun, even if they don't truly understand what the concept is or how it works; the overprotective parent who has all the stop signs and no solutions. Yes, I have heard them all, and unfortunately, consumers tend to listen to this as advice, but the reality is that it is most often bad advice because it comes from a place of ignorance.

Ask yourself, would you fly in a plane engineered by someone who has never built planes? Would you allow your knee surgery to be done by someone who wasn't a board-certified surgeon? The answer to both questions is a resounding "no," so why do we take financial advice from those who aren't qualified to give it?

One of the most important things I could have you take from this book is the idea that only a financial rating company is qualified to evaluate your insurance or annuity company. The four primary rating companies in the United States are Standard & Poor's, Moody's, Fitch, & AM Best. These agencies are allowed inside access to a company's financial status and provide insight as to the likelihood of the insurance or annuity company being around in the next ten or twenty years and beyond.

Yes, the financial rating agencies took some heat in the 2008 banking meltdown, but the complications of rating banks are far more difficult than rating insurance and annuity companies. Ultimately, it all comes back to what types of investments they have made, how many liabilities they have on the books, and what sort of reserves they have, along with their ongoing business influx.

When an annuity or life insurance company has an "Excellent" rating, they are in a great position to honor their guarantee. When you combine those guarantees with the presence of re-insurance and the additional safeguard solution of the state guarantee fund, annuity companies are setup to better guarantee your retirement when compared to public stock companies that people purchase inside their IRA without batting an eye.

The Internet can be one of our best and worst sources for information when conducting research. Google any company and type in "complaints" after it, and you will inevitably get complaints. Go ahead, try it. Type in a company name, followed by "complaints," and you will get a list of complaints against that company. Here are two reasons why this is a bad idea:

1. Most complaints stem from clients who are simply frustrated with customer support or were misinformed by their sales representative. These complaints are often laced with emotion and have nothing to do with the features or servicing of the product, but with the expectations of the client, which were misguided from the beginning. On the other hand, there are also occasional instances where the consumer is now in a different financial position. Perhaps they have a financial emergency or a change of heart, and they decide that if they complain they might get something for their perceived trouble.

2. When we are searching for something, we will find it. This is a phenomenon called *confirmation bias*.

This means that if we already believe something to be true, we will keep searching or interpret the search results to support our theory.

If you are an agent or an advisor who is being subjected to a complaint, I suggest you hit the pause button, rewind, and review with the client what it was they wanted when they first purchased the product you recommended. Oftentimes, humans need things to be repeated because change is uncomfortable, even if it puts us in a better position than before.

If you are a consumer and you find yourself searching online for a complaint against the company you are considering buying from, I suggest you stop and ask yourself, "Do they have an A- or higher financial rating?" If they do, then why are you looking? Is there something about the agent or advisor selling the annuity that you don't trust? If the answer is no, then take a moment to acknowledge the fact that you might just be recognizing change and know that change is uncomfortable and you might instinctually fight it, even if it is improving your situation. So, if the company has a strong rating, and you believe in your agent and believe that the solution they are providing is putting you in a better place, then there is a good chance that everything is fine and you are just uncomfortable with the change, not the solution.

Beware of the Better Business Bureau: One of the most common mistakes consumers make when researching a financial product is relying on the Better Business Bureau (BBB).

The BBB has no financial insight into the companies they grade. They do not have a background as to the historical balance sheets of insurance or annuity companies, and they don't even look at claims' records or volume of payout information. The BBB says on their own website, "BBB ratings represent the BBB's opinion of how the business is likely to interact with their customers." The entire rating is based on consumer complaints and has nothing to do with financial strength, claims history, payouts, or CSI scores.

As I stated earlier, most complaints are forged through agent mistakes or consumer ignorance and have nothing to do with the company receiving the complaint. Furthermore, the BBB has potentially exhibited a "pay-to-play" aspect that only allows companies to improve their ratings if they pay for membership.

In 2010, ABC News reported that a Los Angeles group of business owners, to prove their point, paid a $425 membership fee to the BBB and received an "A-" rating for their made-up terrorist entity, Hamas (named after the actual terrorist sect)! Knowing this, can you really allow the BBB to be an authority on which company should manage your nest-egg?

Stick to the financial rating companies and make sure all features of the financial product you are looking at are explained to you and understood, no matter how many times you have to ask. If you need verification or would like a second opinion, my suggestion is to call the company with the representative and ask those questions on a recorded line. The reason I suggest this is because the representative who works there has been trained to have enough product knowledge to answer questions, but at the same time they would not intentionally lie on a recorded line because that lie could be far too costly to the overall company.

Benefit Three – Tax Deferred Growth

There are only two things guaranteed in life: death and taxes. As Americans, we are consumed with finding ways to defer our death, including eating health foods, buying vitamins, and participating in exercise programs, but when was the last time you considered how to defer your taxes?

Annuities have a very powerful and unique benefit that other non-qualified investments don't have, and that is something called *tax deferred growth*. Tax deferral is a simple concept. It means that instead of paying taxes each year on the interest that you earn, such as you do with interest earned on a bank CD, you can defer that tax (penalty free) until a later time. The resulting phenomenon is something we call *triple compounding interest*. With triple compounding interest, we earn our interest, we earn interest on our interest (normal compounding), and we earn interest on the money that would have normally been paid out for taxes. As a result, we can accumulate more money over time when compared to income that is taxed every tax year.

$18,385

$144,504

$162,889

TAXED ACCOUNT   TAX DEFERRED

Assuming a 25% tax bracket and 5% annual gain, a $100,000 FIA would have 12% more after 10 years when compared to a non-tax deferred investment, such as a bank CD

There are a few things to note when it comes to this tax deferred benefit to FIAs. First, if you purchase an FIA with non-qualified funds (funds outside an IRA or qualified defined contribution plan), then you are potentially subjected to a 10% penalty tax on any gains inside that FIA if you withdraw them prior to age of 59.5. This rule was put into place to promote and encourage annuities as a long-term investment vehicle that benefits retirees in the face of declining Social Security workers' contributions (review Retirement Challenges). If you do take out funds prior to age 59.5 on a non-qualified annuity, then you will pay the same 10% penalty tax as you would if you withdrew the funds prematurely from a qualified account (like a 401(k) or IRA). It is important to note that this penalty is only on the interest credited, not on the original principle.

> **Rule 72 Q:** There is one exception to the above 10% penalty tax rule, and that exception is called *Rule 72 Q*. To simplify the explanation of this rule, it states that you can access the funds in your non-qualified annuity (which have grown tax-deferred) without suffering a 10% penalty if you take a stream of "equal and systematic payments." These payments can be the result of when we convert the annuity into lifetime annuity payments, or the result of equal systematic withdrawals for at least five years. Either way, this is one exception to the penalty. Since annuities are tools for long-term plans, they are often used for lifetime or sustained periods of income generation. That would make them perfect candidates for Rule 72 Q in many instances. This rule can also apply to qualified annuities and IRAs, in which case it is referred to as Rule 72 T.

Keep in mind that most Americans who are looking at retirement are accumulating the majority of their retirement funds in some form of a defined contribution plan (401(k), 403(b), 457, etc.), and therefore they are already planning on not touching the funds until age 59.5 or later.

Benefit Four — Elimination of Fees

It has been famously said, "You can't control the market, but you can control what you pay to access it." In my opinion, there are few statements that carry more weight when it comes to retirement planning and overall investment advice.

Exposing hidden fees inside your average investor's portfolio has turned into a life-long mission for me. I want to educate Americans and protect them from unnecessary fees, so this book, and this chapter, are an initial foray into that agenda. However, this topic is a behemoth, and could be its own book. In fact, there have been many books on the topic, and I would recommend that you check out *The Little Book of Common Sense Investing*, written by Vanguard Founder, John C. Bogle. For now, I'll try to keep this brief, factual, and informative, but understand that this topic is of great importance to you for protecting and maximizing your retirement nest-egg.

Let me ask you, have you heard of a load fee or deferred load fee? How about something called a 12b-1 charge? Do you know what an expense ratio is? This list of fees associated with investment funds, like mutual funds, are on top of any management fee that might be charged by a financial advisor, yet most Americans have no idea they exist. These insidious fees are eroding your nest-egg every year and taking tens of thousands of dollars out of your retirement.

There are two basic types of funds for us to invest in: *managed* and *indexed*. Managed funds are just that: funds that have direct management driving decisions on what the fund should buy and sell, and when it should buy and sell. Managed funds are more expensive to run, so they are the funds where investors will find the most fees. Index funds are designed as unmanaged, or *passive* funds. They are not attempting to beat the market, simply to *match* the market. As a result, they are usually stripped of the fees found in managed funds and normally only have a low annual expense ratio. The graphic below demonstrates the difference in expense ratios (an annual fee that is charged to run the fund) between a managed fund and an index fund, according to a study by the Investment Company Institute.

Average Annual Expense Ratios by Fund Type

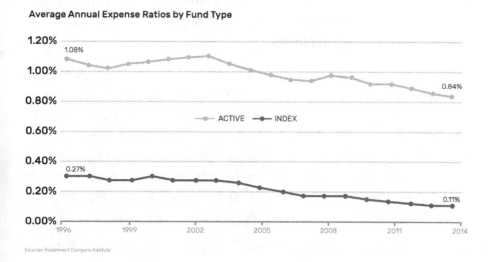

When you combine the annual 12b-1 fee (more on those in a moment) of 0.25 bps that most managed funds have, you have a total and annual difference of 0.98% more in fees that managed funds charge over index funds. If you have a retirement account of $300,000 exposed to these extra fees, it will amount to $2,940 a year, or a whopping $88,200 after thirty years! How long did it take you to save $88,200? How valuable would $88,200 be to you in retirement? What kind of boat, or classic car, or vacation could you buy with $88,200? How much would your surviving spouse or children benefit from an extra $88,200?

To make matters worse, this is not even considering the load fees (or sometimes deferred load fees), which are charged at the time many managed mutual funds are purchased. According to TheBalance.com, these load fees average an eye-popping 5%, and will be charged anytime a new load-fee mutual fund is purchased.

So, what are these load fees and what are they for? Load fees are a one-time charge to the investor to "access" or "enter" the fund. I have heard many financial advisors sell load fees with the pitch, "Wouldn't you rather pay the fee on the seed and not the harvest?" This would make sense if it were not for the fact that you don't have to pay the fee at all! It is no surprise that funds that charge a load fee are also the funds that pay higher commissions to the financial advisor who sold them.

This is why I chose to become a Investment Advisor Representative (IAR) rather than an agent of a broker-dealer. IARs *cannot* receive commissions from any securities product (stocks, bonds, mutual funds, ETFs, etc.). An agent of a broker-dealer *can* receive commissions, and as a result, they might be tempted to place their clients' money into these managed funds to receive a commission, even when the statistics show that managed funds underperform index funds!

And how about those 12b-1 fees I mentioned? The 12b-1 fee is usually .25% per year, because if it were any higher, it would be considered another form of a load fee. Investopedia cites, "A 12b-1 fee is an annual marketing or distribution fee on a mutual fund. The 12b-1 fee is considered to be an operational expense." So, in short, the 12b-1 fee is simply there to help the fund pay to market and advertise to certain financial advisors. The 12b-1 fee does nothing to improve the performance of the fund, and creates "fee drag," which hurts the returns to the investor.

0.25% does not seem like a lot, but it is avoidable, so why pay it? Most index funds do not charge a 12b-1 fee, and when given the choice, I believe everyone would choose not to have that charge. When we look at this number over time, we see that it adds up to a significant amount. If you had $500,000 that was exposed to a 12b-1 fee of .25% every year, that would be $1,250 a year and $12,500 over the course of ten years. Just like our excessive expense ratios previously mentioned, wouldn't you prefer that money stay in your fund and earn interest, or take it for yourself?

Now, if there were some sort of proven return increase for the fees that are charged in managed funds, I'd be all in favor of them. Unfortunately, it is the exact opposite that is true. A report cited in NerdWallet.com stated, "History has shown that it's extremely difficult to beat passive market returns (a.k.a. indexes) year in and year out. In fact, for the fifteen years ending in December 2016, more than 90% of U.S. large-cap, mid-cap and small-cap funds helmed by managers did worse than the S&P 500, according to S&P Dow Indices data".

Another report published on CNBC stated, "While a fund manager may outperform for a year or two, the outperformance does not persist. After ten years, 85% of large-cap funds underperformed the S&P 500, and after fifteen years, nearly 92% are trailing the index".

There are countless articles, studies, and reports that decisively prove that indexed funds outperform actively managed funds over time. The primary reason for this competitive advantage is because of the fees that are in managed funds and not in indexed funds. Fixed indexed annuities are spread products, not fee products, so they, like indexed funds, save clients' money because they do not have fees. Once again, that greed factor of a financial advisor receiving a commission can come into play and result in the recommendation of purchasing an expensive actively managed fund rather than an inexpensive index fund because it pays the advisor more.

This sounds egregious, but it is true. How can you avoid this? One way is to ask your advisor directly if they are advising that you purchase a managed fund or index fund. If they say "managed," then ask them why. If they say that it will beat the index fund, then ask them to prove it, and statistically, you will not find managed funds that beat the market on a consistent basis. In fact, the graphic below from the annual SPIVA report shows how index funds have outperformed managed funds nearly 90% of the time over the past fifteen years. So why would you choose managed funds for your retirement? (for more information on this, please visit https://www. spglobal.com/spdji/en/spiva/#/)

Active Funds vs. Their Benchmarks: U.S Equity
15 Years (1/1/2005 - 12/31/2019)

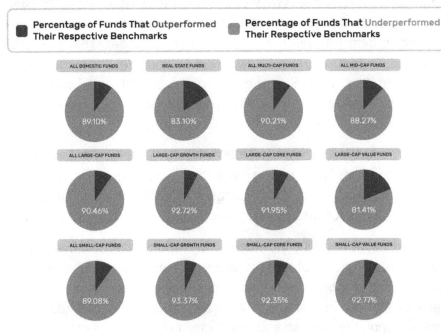

The above graphic shows how managed funds have underperformed against the index over the past fifteen years. So ask yourself, which of these do I own and why would I pay fees to underperform?

One other approach would be looking at the type of advisor you are using. An advisor who is an agent and works for a broker-dealer has a suitability duty, which simply means that they must make sure the product is suitable, but not that it's the *best* product for your needs. An advisor who is a Investment Advisor Representative is held to a fiduciary standard and must choose the product that is in your best interest. As stated before, Investment Advisor Representative also cannot collect commissions on securities, so they are not swayed by that temptation.

I know many of you are asking, "Where do licensed insurance agents fall in this equation?" They are also held to a suitability standard (although best-interest standards are on their way) and they receive a commission on the annuity that is sold, but the commission comes out of the spread from the annuity company, not from your funds, which most clients would prefer. This does not insulate them from the temptation to sell you a product that pays them the most commission or helps them qualify for a vacation, but since 2016, that landscape has drastically changed, and commissions have become more normalized, creating far less temptation to push one annuity product over another.

It is also important to point out that the vast majority of FIAs and annuities available to the public are constructed to pay out a commission. There are some commission-free annuities being developed (specifically targeting use by Registered Investment Advisors), but currently there are so few they really are not a viable option. In the future, I would predict there will be more, and that could only benefit the consumer.

In other words, an insurance agent who sells you an annuity is making a commission, but they would make a commission on any annuity they sold, and those commissions no longer vary dramatically from one carrier to the other, and the agent does not have any viable options of annuities they could sell that *do not* pay a commission. When we contrast that with a securities agent who is choosing to sell you a managed fund, they are choosing (in most cases) to sell you something that is historically inferior in performance to an index fund and the only guarantee is that it will cost you more in fees and pay them a higher commission. These are facts.

Personally, I think all commissions should be normalized and discussed clearly, whether it is a securities product or annuity. I also believe that agents and advisors receiving incentive trips in the insurance industry should be banned, just like they are in the securities industry, because it *can* have the potential to sway the decision on which product to choose. I say this and I have received such trips! Why would I suggest this and participate in the trips that are offered as incentives? Because I know that as a fiduciary, I am always putting the client in the best annuity for their situation, and not basing my recommendations on commission or trip incentive.

How does all this relate to fixed indexed annuities? FIAs do not charge fees. Oftentimes, consumers get these products confused with the fee-heavy variable annuities, but FIAs are not securities products and do not have those same fees. When you invest in an FIA, you are investing in a spread product, not a fee product, so you are eliminating fees from the equation.

In some instances, there can be a charge to your FIA, but these are *optional* charges that give you something in return for the charge. Unlike a load fee or 12b-1, where the fee simply goes to pay the management and overhead and marketing, any charge inside an FIA that you elect to pay will give you something in return. For example, if you purchase a basic safe-growth accumulation FIA that you can withdraw 5% a year from, you might want additional liquidity and guarantees, so you can elect to pay 0.95% a year and now you will receive a higher upfront bonus, you can withdraw up to 20% each year, and you have a return-of-premium clause in year four added to your annuity contract.

In another example, you might have an annuity that you add a 0.30% annual charge to, but in return, you will receive a 30% increase to the death benefit when the annuitant dies.

Benefit	Without Optional Charge	With Optional Charge
Up-front Bonus	5%	9%
Maximum Amount Withdrawn Per Year	5%	10%
Death Benefit	Account Value	Account Value +30%

anonymous FIA riders and benefits

These are just two of the many examples of additional rider charges that can be elected for your FIAs to customize them if needed. For those who are thinking, "Aha! That's where they get you!" you are wrong. I have sold millions of dollars of FIAs and over 90% of mine do not have any rider charges on them. In fact, all the seven benefits of FIAs for retirement are offered without any charges, which shows you the power of these financial tools. Furthermore, I have never encountered an FIA that pays a higher commission for more fees added, so there is no incentive for the agent to sell them.

Look at the graphic below. You can see real numbers representing how fees can erode your retirement. These same fees can be avoided with an FIA.

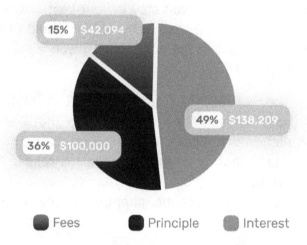

Fees   Principle   Interest

Above graph shows amount lost to fees of 1.50% over 20 years on a $100,000 investment earning 5%.

We can't control the market, but we can control the fees we pay. Many of us are unaware what fees we are being charged and how it is eroding our nest-egg. FIAs can eliminate the fees seen in traditional equity investments, such as load fees, expense fees and 12b-1 fees. According to the Investment Company Institute, the average annual fees (expense ratio & 12b-1) for equity mutual funds were 1.50% per year. These fees, which offer no guarantee, can erode a substantial amount of your retirement overtime.

In summary, there are many things you have little control of when it comes to your retirement. You might have great health or poor health. You might live through an economic boom or bust. The market might go up or it might go down. Managing the fees you have in retirement is controllable, and an FIA allows you that control by eliminating fees.

Benefit Five – Elimination of Market Risk

If you were boarding an airplane and the pilot announced over the intercom, "Folks, we have a 22% chance of going down in a fiery ball of flames today," would you stay in your seat or would you get up and walk off the plane? Chances are, you would find your way to the nearest exit and never travel on a plane again. Where am I drawing this comparison from?

Since 1950, the S&P 500 has gone down 22.8% of the time (16 out of 70) years. Those who know me know that I am a patriot and a capitalist, and I believe in the U.S. stock market, so I am not citing these statistics to evoke fear in the reader. I am citing them because when it comes to your retirement, any down market can result in a drastic change for the worse in your lifestyle.

I also realize that crashing in an airplane, which results in almost guaranteed death, is not the same as having the market go down, but when you are in retirement, it can certainly feel as helpless. I am drawing this comparison because I believe that too many Americans enter their retirement blindly and have no idea how much risk they are subjected to. They also take on this risk without a reason or a set goal on what value they want their retirement to reach and what they want to use the money for. They are also unaware of alternatives to this risk.

There is a real risk called *sequence of returns* risk (SOR), which has to do with the order in which your returns come, not what the overall average return of your portfolio is. If the order of your investment returns is in the wrong sequence while withdrawing money to live on in retirement, then you can find yourself running out of money too early, despite having attractive overall average annual returns to your portfolio.

Look at the two portfolios below. These portfolios represent 60%/40% stock bond splits from actual historical periods in time. The first one is from 1969 for thirty years and the second one is from 1979 for thirty years. The clients are labeled Mr. Smith and Ms. Jones, respectively. Notice that Mr. Smith has a higher average annual return at 10.5%. Incredibly, he also only has four years with negative returns (talk about timing the market right!), compared to 26 years where the market is up. If someone told me I'm going to have thirty years of retirement and I'm going to average 10.5% per year, only have four down years, and the remaining years being positive, I would jump on that as my retirement scenario! But remember, you are no longer putting money *into* your retirement and you are now taking money *out* of your retirement. As you can see below, even with that fantastic performance, because he is withdrawing 5% a year and because his negative returns happen early in his retirement, he would run out of money by the time he was 84.

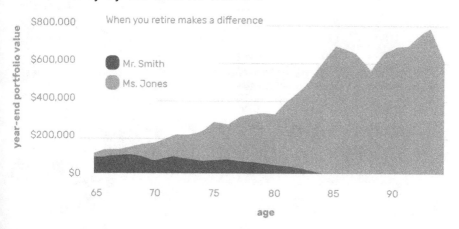

Mr. Smith

investment: $100,000
Stocks 60% | bonds 40%
Retired 1/1/1969 - annual withdrawals: $5,0000

Age	year	ror	year-end value
65	1969	-2.6%	$92,168
66	1970	5.3%	$91,446
67	1971	10.5%	$95,219
68	1972	12.9%	$101,447
69	1973	-6.6%	$88,410
70	1974	-12.6%	$70,219
71	1975	25.1%	$80,085
72	1976	16.5%	$85,107
73	1977	-2.4%	$74,324
74	1978	6.3%	$69,660
75	1979	14.7%	$69,487
76	1980	23.9%	$74,222
77	1981	3.4%	$63,670
78	1982	16.6%	$60,391
79	1983	16.6%	$56,145
80	1984	7.3%	$45,480
81	1985	22.0%	$40,198
82	1986	13.9%	$30,286
83	1987	5.7%	$15,941
84	1988	12.2%	$1,176
85	1989	22.1%	Exhausted
86	1990	1.2%	Exhausted
87	1991	20.8%	Exhausted
88	1992	6.1%	Exhausted
89	1993	7.3%	Exhausted
90	1994	2.0%	Exhausted
91	1995	24.6%	Exhausted
92	1996	16.3%	Exhausted
93	1997	21.1%	Exhausted
94	1998	19.1%	Exhausted

Average ror
10.5%

Ms. Jones

investment: $100,000
Stocks 60% | bonds 40%
Retired 1/1/1979 - annual withdrawals: $5,0000

year	ror	year-end value
1979	14.%	$109,172
1980	23.9%	$128,899
1981	3.4%	$126,282
1982	16.6%	$139,848
1983	16.6%	$155,426
1984	7.3%	$158,880
1985	22.0%	$185,630
1986	13.9%	$203,223
1987	5.7%	$206,232
1988	12.2%	$222,537
1989	22.1%	$262,402
1990	1.2%	$255,753
1991	20.8%	$298,808
1992	6.1%	$306,574
1993	7.3%	$318,026
1994	2.0%	$313,351
1995	24.6%	$378,884
1996	16.3%	$429,072
1997	21.1%	$507,502
1998	19.1%	$592,094
1999	14.3%	$664,249
2000	-0.8%	$645,969
2001	-3.8%	$608,120
2002	-9.3%	$538,413
2003	18.9%	$626,319
2004	8.2%	$663,790
2005	3.8%	$674,761
2006	11.2%	$735,149
2007	6.1%	$764,278
2008	-20.5%	$591,402

Average ror
9.6%

Considering people these days have better access to health care, have more advanced medical treatments, and are living longer than ever before, I don't like the prospects of having to die before eighty-four or running out of money completely. Obviously, this could work the other way, and the returns could come early in retirement and create a surplus, but we really have no way of knowing. You must ask yourself: Is it worth the risk? Unfortunately, too many Americans are not even aware of this risk, and too many of their advisors are not preparing for it, potentially because they can make more money keeping their client's assets in equities.

An FIA offers two things that can avoid sequence of returns risk. First, the FIA will never participate in down markets, so your retirement will not experience negative returns. Second, those who activate the lifetime income feature of their FIAs (income rider or annuitization) are not affected by down markets and they will receive a lifetime payout for as long as they or their spouse lives, depending on how they structure the annuity payout. Either way you choose, the benefit of the FIA for avoiding sequence of returns risk is clear.

Benefit Six – Guaranteed Lifetime Income

Offering a stream of lifetime payments in return for some sort of service or investment dates to the early Roman Empire. Annuities for lifetime income began in the United States around the year 1720 with the Presbyterian Church. The idea was very simple: Money would be set aside and orphans or pastors who needed money in retirement if they did not have income would be paid an income stream. This staple feature of annuities is what they are known best for and true lifetime income guarantees are unique to annuities. Yes, annuities are the *only* retirement product that can guarantee lifetime income.

How do annuities accomplish this? Where most stock investments or bond ladders use principal and interest (or yield) to create a stream of income, annuities use a third dimension called mortality credits. These mortality credits represent money that has been set aside by the annuity company to pay those who are in the mortality pool (those clients who are due a lifetime income payment). The older the consumer is, the more money they get allocated from this mortality pool—this is called a *mortality credit*. As a result, even if the principal and interest has completely declined to zero, the lifetime annuity payments to the annuitant will be guaranteed because of these mortality credits.

The graphic below shows you the third dimension of mortality credit and how effectively it can guarantee payments no matter how long an annuitant lives.

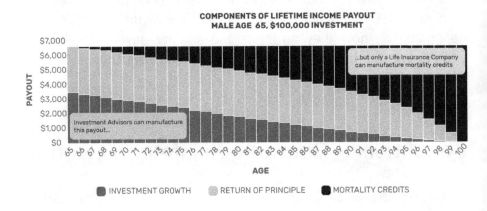

Did you know that annuities can help you live longer? It's true. In an article published in the *Journal of Financial Service Professionals*, Patrick C. Tricker, JD, MSF references a study when he notes, "It is well established that individuals who annuitize their retirement savings tend to live longer than the general population. In the United States, a 65-year-old male who purchases a life annuity can expect to live about 20% percent longer than a 65-year-old male who does not" (Tricker 2018, 43-50).

A 20% longer lifespan when you have an annuity? Obviously, there is going to be some self-selection here because those who *expect* to live longer are more likely to purchase an annuity. However, those who purchase an annuity are also more likely to *want* to live longer, and can pay more attention to their eating habits, exercise regimen, and overall health. So, yes, annuities can help you live longer!

Annuities with lifetime income can also make you happier in retirement. In a 2018 Guaranteed Lifetime Income Study, conducted by Greenwald & Associates and CANNEX, respondents said the greatest benefits of having a protected lifetime income are protection against longevity risk, peace of mind, and being better able to budget—all of which can make for a less stressful and happier overall retirement.

Between 1998 and 2010, the University of Michigan conducted the Health and Retirement Study. The results revealed that satisfaction scores for the 26,000 individuals in the study were significantly higher for people who had more than 30% of their assets invested in protected lifetime income products (annuities) (Greenwald & Associates 2012).

Guaranteed lifetime income can be especially valuable during times of political upheaval and stock market recessions. Or, in situations where there are outside factors affecting our daily living, such as the Covid-19 pandemic. In fact, 2020 illustrates a year where someone who is receiving guaranteed lifetime income would probably sleep far better than someone who isn't!

Many people call annuities *longevity risk insurance* and when it comes to guaranteed lifetime income, this is very true. Living too long can be a severe risk in retirement. As discussed earlier in the chapter on Retirement Challenges, a longer lifespan exacerbates all the retirement challenges—and for many Americans, running out of money is a real and very scary possibility. Those who have an annuity will not have to worry about this. The annuity with the mortality credits is guaranteed to pay you for life.

Did you know that Social Security is a form of an annuity? Social Security payments last for as long as the entitled recipient lives. Their payment is a result of what they have paid into Social Security during their working years (think of that as their premium), and the longer they wait to receive their Social Security payment, the higher their payment will be (those are called longevity credits). And when you die, your spouse will receive your payment (assuming it is the higher of the two they are eligible for). The same thing can be said about a pension, and both instances are simply different forms of an annuity.

According to a 2015 study by Transamerica Center for Retirement Studies, 41% of Americans said their biggest retirement fear was running out of money in retirement. What would your answer be? If you are over 60, chances are high that running out of money in retirement is somewhere near the top. Only life insurance and annuity companies can offer these guarantees because they are on both sides of the mortality risk. The longer we as Americans live, the longer the insurance companies will pay us. For every dollar of guaranteed annuity payments they have to send out, they have a dollar of life insurance premium coming in. This puts insurance companies in a unique and favorable position to have a hedge against mortality and is why no other entity can offer an annuity.

Think about it, what we're used to in life is earning a paycheck and spending the paycheck. When it comes to retirement, many of us do not have a plan, but it would make sense to try and replicate the lifestyle we've become accustomed to for so many decades and create a way for us to receive that monthly paycheck. The foundation of every retirement plan should be creating a healthy guaranteed lifetime payment. This can be done with Social Security, pensions, and annuities.

How you create lifetime income from an annuity, or more specifically a fixed indexed annuity, can vary and will be discussed later in the chapter called *FIAs in Action*, but the reason you create lifetime income from an annuity goes to the core of creating a happy and enjoyable retirement. As my friend Tom Hegna, a renowned retirement expert, has said, you must either spend the money or give it away. You can't take it with you. Far too many of us are leery of converting our retirement nest-egg into lifetime income because we are afraid to part ways with it. A fixed indexed annuity is a fantastic option because it allows for the ability to receive lifetime income payments, but still access your principal in an emergency. This flexibility is key to the benefit of lifetime income from an FIA.

Benefit Seven – Avoidance of Probate

When is the last time you thought about probate? Chances are the answer is never. This is why it is so important to consider how probate can impact your retirement nest-egg when you die. For many of us, we might not really understand what probate is and how it works, so let's start there.

In short, probate is the legal process of deciding how to distribute one's assets when they are deceased. If the deceased has a will, the probate court will look to that document first, and if they don't have a will, which is called dying *intestate*, then the court needs to interpret the law and make the decisions on behalf of the deceased. This process does cost money and can vary based on where you live. For small estates, the cost of quick probate can be relatively small, maybe a few hundred dollars, but for many estates, the cost is a percentage of your estate. According to LegalZoom, the average probate cost in the United States is somewhere between 2% and 4%, with some states reaching as high as 7%.

So, in theory you can assume that if you died with $3,000,000 going to probate, it could cost you up to $210,000 to have it settled and distributed to your loved ones.

I have been in this business for a while and I've seen my share of people who really don't care about anyone other than themselves.

I don't mean that cynically. There are simply some people who are just too estranged from their family or who do not have any family or loved ones whatsoever to leave their inheritance to. I have also stated that the number one rule is to take care of yourself. It's your money that you've earned so make sure you take care of yourself first. In other words, make sure you live the retirement you worked so hard for!

That being said, the majority of people truly desire to leave money to their loved ones when they die. If we know that probate costs can reach as high as 7% of our estate, and you had $500,000 passing on to your loved ones through probate, then you could potentially be losing $35,000 through the probate court system. Ask yourself, what does $35,000 mean to you? How much time did it take for you to earn $35,000? How much blood, sweat, and tears went into that $35,000? Wouldn't you rather have the $35,000 go to your loved ones or a charity rather than the probate court? All these questions are rhetorical because we would all rather avoid paying money at probate.

An FIA avoids probate and pays your death proceeds directly to a beneficiary or multiple beneficiaries, even if that beneficiary is a trust. This benefit of an FIA is not exclusive to FIAs, but it is a very valuable benefit that should always be considered for its value.

Seven Benefits Summary

Now that you understand the Seven Benefits of FIAs for Retirement, it is important to point out that all of these benefits come with all FIAs free of charge. You can see why FIAs are the fastest growing segment of annuities sold today. They are truly a turnkey retirement tool that can prepare you for the retirement challenges we face. Since we don't know exactly which challenge will show up next in retirement, the FIA has tremendous appeal to those who want to be prepared for anything!

CHAPTER VI

THE IMPORTANCE OF SOCIAL SECURITY PLANNING

According to Motley Fool, in 2019 the average IRA balance in America was $115,400 and the average home value was $284,600. These numbers probably don't surprise you, but what might surprise you is how small they are compared to the average Social Security benefit collected during a person's retirement.

According to the Social Security Administration, the average monthly Social Security benefit is $1,503. So, if someone collected Social Security for twenty years, they would most likely exceed $400,000 in their lifetime when we account for CPI adjustments. If they live to be ninety, then the benefit could surpass $500,000, and if passed on to their spouse, it could reach even higher. This means that, for many American retirees, Social Security is their most valuable retirement asset. Unfortunately, it is the one that we probably understand the least and utilize the worst.

There are many facets of Social Security and Social Security income planning, and certain scenarios can become quite in depth, but the majority of proper planning and optimization can come from simply slowing down and looking at your situation before you decide when you are going to claim your benefit. That is what I want to accomplish in this chapter. We will do this by first learning what

Social Security is and where it is headed, then some of the rules and how to properly decide what is best for you and your family.

Social Security Isn't Going Away

Ask some of your friends and family, "When should someone take their Social Security benefits?" Inevitably, there will be more than one person who exclaims "As soon as you can!" and their justification for that has something to do with the "fact" that Social Security is underfunded and going away. Well, this is only partially true, and very far from the reality.

Social Security is arguably the most important civil benefit in the United States of America. Without Social Security payments, over 64,000,000 people could fall into destitution and the economy would be affected worse than any other recessions in history. Yes, Social Security is underfunded, but this is a bit misunderstood.

Many news reports claim that the Social Security Trust Fund is going to dry up! In fact, many reports estimate this will happen as soon as 2034, but what most people do not understand is that even with the Social Security Trust Fund completely depleted, the Social Security program would continue to operate, and without any modifications, it would be able to fund the program with recipients still receiving *most* of their benefits. For most people, their benefits are paid from deductions in payroll taxes, not from the Social Security Trust Fund. Furthermore, small tweaks and changes can shift the tide and ensure that the trust fund will not run out.

Think of it this way: If the military were over budget, and we were in the midst of fighting a war, do you think the nation would simply stop fighting? It is absurd to even think that would be acceptable. Social Security is every bit as important as our nation's defense, so why would it be any different? Will Social Security undergo changes in the future? Yes. Will these changes affect our grandchildren? Yes, but as we live longer and work longer, these changes will probably seem as fluid as they have been since Social Security started over 85 years ago.

The Basics

Social Security was created in 1935 to help pay for the elderly Americans who could no longer earn a living. It is important to understand that you must earn forty working credits to be eligible for a Social Security payment. You earn credits when you work and pay Social Security taxes. The number of credits does not affect the amount of benefits you receive. It only determines if you are eligible or not. You do not get extra benefits for earning more than the minimum number of credits.

If you are eligible, then the amount of your payment is determined by the amount you earned (and paid into the Social Security fund) over your work history. As of 2020, the maximum benefit someone can receive at age 66 is $3,011 per month.

Social Security benefits can be claimed as early as age 62 and deferred to age 70. If you defer your payments, you will receive more. In fact, you will receive roughly an 8% compounding increase each year you delay your Social Security benefit. As an example, take a look at my projected Social Security benefit. If I defer my Social Security check to age 70, it will almost double from what I would get paid at age 62.

If you look at this mathematically, any beneficiary who plans on living past age 78 should wait until age 67 to take their Social Security paycheck. However, according to MoneyTalks, nearly 35% of men and nearly 40% of women take their benefit at age 62, when they are first eligible for it. Why is that? The reason most Americans take their Social Security early is because they want or need the money immediately, or they believe or

Social Security Benefits
Early - Full - Delayed

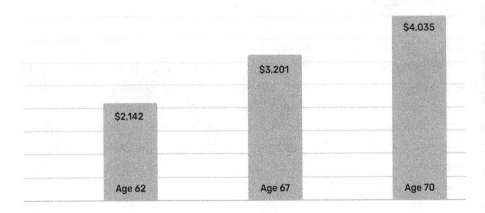

have been told that the money could run out (as we previously discussed in this chapter). This is truly unfortunate and could be corrected with some basic education and discipline.

We need to look at retirement in totality. We need to understand that it is a marathon, not a sprint, and that taking your Social Security at age 62 is only a good idea if you don't plan on being alive (or having a spouse survive you) fifteen years later. For those who do plan on being alive at 78 and beyond, they need to be looking at how they can defer their Social Security. Take a look at the graphic below and you can see it in plain math. If you defer your benefit, you will have a higher monthly payment once you do elect to take it, but you will have "lost income" to make up for. The number of years needed to make up for the "lost income" is known as the break-even point, and for someone who deferred their Social Security payment to age 67, they would need to live 11.7 years (or to about age 79) to break even. Every payment after that would be a gain.

AGE AT WHICH YOU CLAIM BENEFITS	TOTAL BENEFITS FORGONE BY WAITING BEYOND 62	INCREASE IN ANNUAL INCOME DUE TO DELAYING BENEFITS CLAIM	YEARS TO BREAK EVEN
62	$0	$0	NM
63	$12,600	$900	14.0
64	$25,200	$1,800	14.0
65	$37,800	$3,000	12.6
66	$50,400	$4,200	12.0
67	$63,000	$5,400	11.7
68	$75,600	$6,840	11.1
69	$88,200	$8,280	10.7
70	$100,800	$9,740	10.3

Understand that you get rewarded for each month, not each year, that you defer. So, even if you must take your social security seventeen months after you are eligible, you are rewarded for that delay, not just at the anniversary of your benefit eligibility.

Because many Americans fear that Social Security is going away, they have a sense of entitlement that leads them to believe that since they paid into the program, they better get their money out before it's gone. This logic is flawed because the money that they paid in is long since spent, and the benefit they are entitled to is being funded by current contributions and future taxation.

Another important factor in understanding Social Security benefits is knowing how it adjusts. Social Security payments have a *cost-of-living adjustment* (COLA) built into them. Since 1975, Social Security benefit payments have been tied to the Consumer Pricing Index of Wage Earners (CPI-W). This means that the benefit payments can increase each year in line with when inflation rises. This is a hugely valuable feature that is difficult to replicate in retirement income planning. If you had a Social Security benefit payment of $1,500 monthly and it adjusted annually at a mere 1.5% per year, by the end of 25 years, that monthly payment is now a whopping $2,144—an increase of 43%. The graphic below shows the recent history of CPI-W increases to Social Security payments. Obviously, we are in a very low inflationary period, but if inflation does climb, so will your Social Security payment.

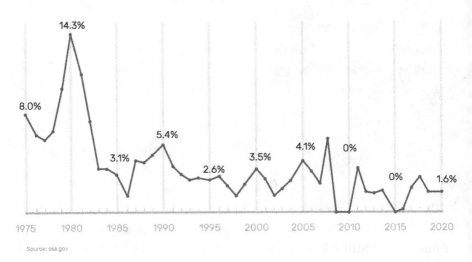

Source: ssa.gov

Another important factor in understanding Social Security payments is understanding that the larger of the two spousal payments will survive to the second living spouse. So, not only does delaying your larger payment increase the total by 8% compounding interest every year, and the annual payment adjusts upward with inflation, the larger payment also has a survivorship clause that passes it onto the longest living partner in a marriage. Therefore, proper planning of this benefit is so important and keeping the long-term goals in mind when making these crucial decisions is paramount.

Yet another important benefit that many people are not even aware of is something called an *exclusion ratio* in a Social Security payment. Now, I know what you might be thinking, "I already paid taxes on my Social Security wages. Why should I have to pay again?" As true as this may be, you still must comply with the IRS, and they will assess taxes on your Social Security wages each year, but there are two things in your favor. First, the calculation to decide how much of your Social Security wages are taxed is something called a *provisional tax* calculation, and it only counts 50% of your Social Security payments against you. The second factor is that even if you are at the highest tax bracket, at least 15% of your Social Security will never be taxed. More on Social Security taxation later in this chapter.

Lastly, understand what your *full retirement age* (FRA) is and what it means. The FRA is the point of Social Security that has been determined as the age that you are "supposed" to take your Social Security. Yes, you can take it earlier, at a penalty, and you can take it later, with a reward, but the FRA is in between those two and has one significant importance for many people planning for retirement, and that is what's called the *earnings test*. The earnings test specifically has to do with how much income you can earn while taking Social Security payments *before* your FRA. This is critical to understand because many Americans are looking for a hybrid retirement (thank you, Tom Hegna), where they take Social Security and still work and earn income. Be careful! If you make more than $18,960 (as of 2021) a year and you are not scheduled to hit your FRA until after 2021, then you will lose a dollar for every two dollars of earnings you have past the exemption amount ($18,960 as of 2021).

For example, if Mrs. Smith is taking her Social Security payment of $1,000 per month ($12,000 a year) at age 64 but her FRA isn't until age 66 and she is working at a department store making $36,000 a year, then she will be reducing the amount of Social Security that she can collect. Here are the calculations.

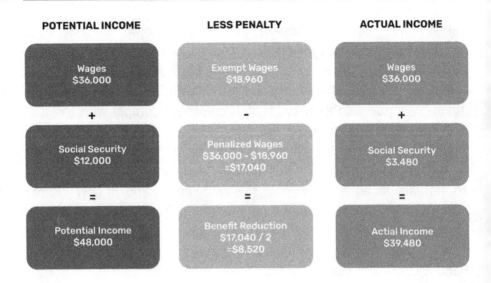

POTENTIAL INCOME	LESS PENALTY	ACTUAL INCOME
Wages $36,000	Exempt Wages $18,960	Wages $36,000
+	-	+
Social Security $12,000	Penalized Wages $36,000 - $18,960 =$17,040	Social Security $3,480
=	=	=
Potential Income $48,000	Benefit Reduction $17,040 / 2 =$8,520	Actial Income $39,480

So, the rule on how the penalty works states that the Social Security Administration will withhold $1 in benefits for every $2 of earnings. This means that if she has $17,040 of non-exempt income, she will lose $1 for every $2 of these earnings. If she divides $17,040 by 2, then we get a reduction of $8,520 from her Social Security.

I have never been one for a free lunch, but I certainly wouldn't want to be working at a job just to reduce my Social Security income by 71%! In the above scenario, the client would have the ability to make the same amount of money working fewer hours if they simply were aware of the rule and didn't accrue working wages past the annual exemption limit.

One caveat to this rule is that if you are working in the year that you are going to turn your FRA, your benefit is only reduced $1 for every $3 of earnings, so in the previous example, she would divide her non-exempt earnings by 3 instead of 2 and have a $5,680 reduction instead of an $8,520 reduction.

So, if you are going to be planning on working in retirement to earn extra income while taking Social Security, plan carefully, as this can be an exercise in futility if you have not reached your FRA and if you plan on earning more than the exemption allows. For many retirees, working in retirement should be a way to *defer* your Social Security, not take both if you have not reached your FRA.

Find Your Social Security Statement

If you are like me, you have a vague recollection of when the government mailed you a Social Security statement each year. Unfortunately, those days are long gone. In 2011, Social Security stopped mailing statements each year and they now only mail statements to those citizens who are age 60+ who have not created an online account. I recommend that you set up an online account at www.ssa.gov/myaccount so you have all the information needed at your fingertips.

Overall, I believe the administration has done a fantastic job with these online accounts. All information is easy to ascertain, they have helpful tools available for you to better understand your benefits, and the security measures are of the highest level to

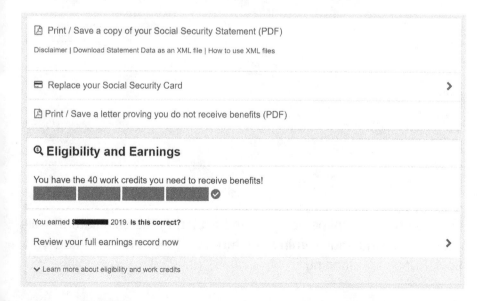

ensure your privacy. The online accounts have records of your earnings history for you to review, so if you see anything amiss, you can report it back to them quickly. I advise everyone to create an online account and review their earnings history.

Take a look at the screenshot below. This is from my online Social Security statement. You can see the easy-to-understand layout, which starts by giving you links to your paper or PDF statement and your work history and credits with a link to your earnings history for you to review.

Below that you will find a very helpful and easy-to-understand interactive graphic (when you are online) that shows you what your benefits will be if you take them early (age 62), on time (age 67), delayed (age 70), or at any point in between.

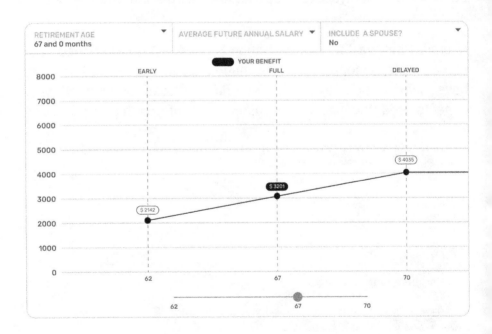

So, creating your online account and exploring the calculators while double-checking your earnings history is a great place to start your Social Security planning.

Minimize Your Social Security Tax Footprint

Many retirees and pre-retirees are not aware of, or have not planned on, how to minimize their tax footprint in retirement. For example, many of us have heard of *Adjusted Gross Income (AGI)* and how that is used to calculate our income tax, but have you heard of *provisional income*? Provisional income is the calculation used to determine how much of your Social Security income is taxed. Unlike AGI, provisional income does count municipal bond income, which is usually purchased because it pays out federally tax free. Misunderstandings like this can have a negative consequence on our tax footprint in retirement. The basic calculation for provisional income is below:

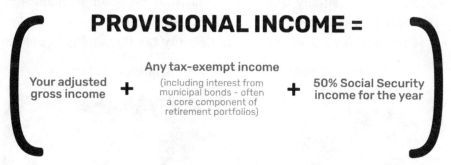

PROVISIONAL INCOME =

(Your adjusted gross income **+** Any tax-exempt income (including interest from municipal bonds - often a core component of retirement portfolios) **+** 50% Social Security income for the year)

Another example of retirement tax planning is when we look at how much money we draw out of our qualified funds (like an IRA) and how that affects our provisional income. Social Security income can be taxed if your overall provisional income reaches a certain "threshold." For example, if Joe Smith is a married, filing jointly, taxpayer and his provisional income is less than $32,000, then none of his Social Security income will be taxed. However, if his provisional income is $40,000, then up to 50% of his Social Security income is subject to income tax. When we look at drawing money out from our IRA, we know that it will count as income, and therefore be included in our provisional income calculation. Using Joe Smith as a hypothetical example again and knowing that Joe Smith (age 68) has wages of $0, tax-exempt bond income of $5,000, and a combined Social Security income of $42,000 (of which we calculate half of it for provisional income), then his provisional income is $26,000 and none of his Social Security income will be subject to taxation. Let us now say that Joe Smith also has an IRA with $350,000 in it. He has planned on this IRA subsidizing his retirement. He wants to go on a vacation to Greece with his wife which will cost $12,000. To pay for the vacation, he decides to take out $12,000 from his IRA. This $12,000 will now be included in his provisional income for that year, raising it to $38,000 and now up to 50% of his Social Security income can have income tax consequences. Knowing this, Joe could have planned better and split the $12,000 withdrawal between his two tax years (like a $6,000 withdrawal on December 20th and another $6,000 withdrawal on January 20th). Knowing that provisional income is used and understanding where the Social Security tax thresholds are is the key. A table of the Social Security tax thresholds is below.

CALCULATING YOUR SOCIAL SECURITY INCOME TAX

Provisional income amounts if you file as:		
AGE AT WHICH YOU CLAIM BENEFITS	TOTAL BENEFITS FORGONE BY WAITING BEYOND 62	YEARS TO BREAK EVEN
Less than $25,000	Less than $32,000	Social Security income is tax-free
$25,000 to $34,00	$32,000 to $44,00	Up to 50% of Social Security income is taxable
More than $34,000	More than $44,000	Up to 85% of Social Security income is taxable

Sources: Congressional Research Service

Be aware of these levels and how to calculate your provisional tax so you can minimize the amount of Social Security that is subject to taxation.

Optimize Your Social Security

Every situation is unique, but if there were one rule that applied to *most* retiring couples, it would be to defer the larger of your two Social Security payments. This simple rule is easy to understand. If there is a married couple, and one of them has a $2,200 Social Security payment due, and the other has a $1,200 Social Security payment due, the higher payment (the one worth $2,200) is the one you want to defer.

How long should you defer it? That depends on your health. In most situations, deferring the larger payment until age 70 is smart, but in certain cases where both spouses are not healthy, then you can adjust down from age 70, but still, you will want to defer the larger of the two payments longer.

The simple reason for this is because the larger of the two payments is the one that survives the first spouse's death. If a surviving spouse is faced with living three, five, or even ten years or more with only one of the Social Security payments they are used to receiving, then they certainly want the one that remains to count as much as possible. Unfortunately, this simple planning point has been missed with so many in retirement. The proof is in the poverty.

According to the Social Security Administration, over 15% of surviving women fall below the poverty level after their spouse's death. Why? It's simply a matter of poor planning, and since women statistically outlive men, we have far too many widows without enough money at the end of their lives. Since roughly 43% of Social Security recipients have claimed their Social Security at age prior to age 65, then the amount that survives and grows with CPI is too small to stand up alone to inflation and cost of living increases. One must imagine that this is not the outcome that the deceased spouse (oftentimes husbands) had desired, but by not being educated on the consequences of not delaying the larger of the two Social Security payments, the surviving spouse can suffer late in retirement.

FIAs Can Help

There are two common ways that fixed indexed annuities can help you optimize your Social Security income planning.

First, FIAs can be used to bridge the income needed to defer one's social security. If a couple has their primary wage earner retiring at age 65, but they want to defer to at least age 67 (or 70), then they face the challenge of having to "bridge" their income for two to five years to optimize their retirement.

A couple in this situation could certainly have their money in the market, but there is no certainty when it comes to stock-based investments, and when you are doing this sort of planning, you need certainty. They could place the money into conservative CDs or money market accounts, but those offer such little return that they will not outpace inflation. They could also use Treasury Bonds, which are backed by the good faith of the U.S. Government, but current yields on those are barely over 1%. It is in these situations where FIAs (and all annuities) can shine. For example, someone who might need $10,000 a year for three years to bridge their Social Security income gap could purchase an FIA and simply do systematic withdrawals for three years and then stop taking withdrawals in year four (saving the rest of the annuity for future income payments, surviving spousal income, end-of-life health care, legacy planning, or any other retirement challenge) without having to worry about losing money in the market.

Say there is a couple, the husband is 60 and the wife is 56. They are in average health, and the husband wants to retire at age 64 while the wife wants to retire at age 68. The husband, who has the larger of the two Social Security benefits, wants to defer taking his Social Security until his FRA (which is 67) so he can ensure that whichever spouse lives longer (presumably the wife) will have the best chance of affording retirement once the other one passes.

The illustration below shows an FIA that they funded with $300,000 at age 60. When the husband turns 64, he retires, and they withdraw $30,000 a year to supplement their income in lieu of taking Social Security. Once the husband turns 67, he activates his Social Security and stops withdrawing funds from the annuity. At age 72, the wife is now 68 and she retires, so they activate the lifetime income feature of the annuity and withdraw an income stream that continues to grow through indexing and will now last for as long as they are alive.

YEAR ENDING	BEGINNING OF YEAR AGE	END OF YEAR AGE	WITHDRAWALS			END OF YEAR NON-GUARANTEED ANNUITY CONTRACT VALUES			
			FREE PARTIAL WITHDRAWALS	LIFETIME INCOME WITHDRAWALS	CUMULATIVE WITHDRAWALS	BENEFIT BASE [1]	ACCUMULATED VALUE	CASH SURRENDER VALUE	DEATH BENEFIT [1]
12/2021	60	61	$0	$0	$0	$360,000	$300,000	$276,700	$300,000
12/2022	61	62	$0	$0	$0	$411,079	$329,188	$302,261	$329,188
12/2023	62	63	$0	$0	$0	$411,079	$329,188	$305,487	$329,188
12/2024	63	64	$0	$0	$0	$467,148	$361,227	$338,246	$361,227
12/2025	64	65	$30,000	$0	$30,000	$428,351	$331,227	$311,721	$331,227
12/2026	65	66	$30,000	$0	$60,000	$440,879	$330,558	$314,184	$330,558
12/2027	66	67	$30,000	$0	$90,000	$400,866	$300,556	$288,656	$300,556
12/2028	67	68	$0	$0	$90,000	$452,094	$329,828	$320,835	$329,828
12/2029	68	69	$0	$0	$90,000	$452,094	$329,828	$323,891	$329,828
12/2030	69	70	$0	$0	$90,000	$508,330	$361,963	$358,673	$361,963
12/2031	70	71	$0	$0	$90,000	$508,330	$361,963	$361,963	$361,963
12/2032	71	72	$0	$0	$90,000	$570,067	$397,241	$397,241	$397,241
12/2033	72	73	$0	$32,494	$122,494	$523,436	$364,748	$364,748	$364,748
12/2034	73	74	$0	$32,494	$154,988	$533,494	$364,648	$364,648	$364,648
12/2035	74	75	$0	$35,662	$190,649	$481,320	$328,986	$328,986	$328,986
12/2036	75	76	$0	$35,662	$226,311	$479,209	$321,932	$321,932	$321,932
12/2037	76	77	$0	$39,140	$265,451	$420,948	$282,794	$282,794	$282,794
12/2038	77	78	$0	$39,140	$304,591	$404,287	$267,424	$267,424	$267,424
12/2039	78	79	$0	$42,959	$347,550	$359,343	$224,465	$224,465	$224,465
12/2041	79	80	$0	$42,959	$390,509	$305,400	$199,221	$199,221	$199,221
12/2041	80	81	$0	$47,151	$437,660	$233,118	$152,070	$152,070	$152,070
12/2042	81	82	$0	$47,151	$484,811	$178,763	$115,162	$115,162	$115,162
12/2043	82	83	$0	$51,755	$536,566	$98,424	$63,407	$63,407	$63,407
12/2044	83	84	$0	$51,755	$588,321	$20,079	$12,791	$12,791	$12,791
12/2045	84	85	$0	$56,810	$645,130	$0	$0	$0	$0

This is a perfect example of how an FIA can be used to help optimize your Social Security by providing income in retirement while you defer your Social Security payment and then more income later to offset inflation, late-in-life health care costs and income loss with death of the first spouse. All these goals are achieved without having to worry about what the market returns are.

Could this also be accomplished through investments in the stock market? Yes, is the short answer, but it could be threatened if the market declined enough in value during the time when withdrawing the money. The illustration above is using a conservative average rate of return of 4.76%, but even if the market went down every year, the FIA would never do worse than 0%, so it can still accomplish the goal (albeit with less money withdrawn at age 72 and beyond). If the money were directly invested into the stock market, the clients' ability to accomplish this goal could be seriously threatened. For most, having safety and security is the foundation of a good retirement plan that you can enjoy!

A second way that a couple can use an annuity to help with Social Security income planning is by purchasing a deferred income FIA, or *deferred income annuity (DIA)*. This is especially helpful for clients who have already made their Social Security income decisions, but realize they are probably facing a shortfall later in retirement when the first spouse dies.

Perhaps there was a couple who had already claimed Social Security. The husband is 72 and the wife is 70. The husband has poor health and is not expected to live past 80. The wife is in excellent health and assumes she will live into her 90s like her mother has. The husband's Social Security is the higher of the two at $1,580 per month and his wife's Social Security benefit is $650 per month. In addition to Social Security, the husband has a pension of $500 per month, but that only passes on to his wife at 50% value, or $250 per month. So, if the husband does die first, which is the most likely scenario based on age and health, then the wife will lose $900 per month, and at a time late in life when inflation is eating at her purchasing power and health care costs can be rising.

The couple has lived with modest means, but they do have some savings and CDs left over from the sale of their house a few years back. They can utilize $120,000 of that money to purchase an FIA with a guaranteed lifetime income rider. The illustration below shows how an FIA with a deferred income rider can guarantee a future payment stream that will offset the loss of income from the husband and help keep the wife out of poverty.

DEFERRAL YEARS	BEGINNING OF YEAR AGE	END OF YEAR AGE	BEGINNING OF YEAR INCOME BASE	INCOME PERCENTAGE	GUARANTEED LIFETIME INCOME WITHDRAWAL	ANNUAL INCOME IF CONFINED *MUST MEET ELIGIBILITY REQUIREMENTS
0	72	73	$ 132,000	4.65%	$ 6,138	$ 12,276*
1	73	74	$ 144,000	4.75%	$ 6,840	$ 13,680
2	74	75	$ 156,000	4.85%	$ 7,566	$ 15,132
3	75	76	$ 168,000	4.95%	$ 8,316	$ 16,632
4	76	77	$ 180,000	5.05%	$ 9,090	$ 18,180
5	77	78	$ 192,000	5.15%	$ 9,888	$ 19,776
6	78	79	$ 204,000	5.25%	$ 10,710	$ 21,420
7	79	80	$ 216,000	5.35%	$ 11,556	$ 23,112
8	80	81	$ 228,000	5.45%	$ 12,426	$ 24,852
9	81	82	$ 240,000	5.55%	$ 13,320	$ 26,640

These are just two of many examples of how FIAs can help with your Social Security planning, even if you have already claimed your benefit.

For many people, Social Security income planning is the most important step in retirement planning. Understanding the basics and learning how to optimize your payments is key, and the certainty, predictability, and guarantees of an annuity offer a great tool to get the job done!

CHAPTER VII

FIAS IN ACTION

In this chapter we are going to look at real-world scenarios and how the FIA can solve certain retirement challenges. We will start by taking a deeper dive into the various uses of FIAs and then display actual cases (names have been changed to protect consumers' identities) where we have used an FIA as part of a consumer's retirement plan. Let's start with a rundown of how FIAs can be used.

FIAs for Accumulation (Safe Growth)

First and foremost, I want to make myself explicitly clear when I say that I do not recommend FIAs, or any other annuity (including variable annuities), for accumulating a sum of money through ongoing, consistent smaller contributions.

In this chapter and throughout this book, when I talk about safe growth and accumulation, I am referring to funds that have already been created, either through long-term investing, inheritance, or perhaps through the sale of a house, business, or even winning the lottery. The most common scenario we are concerned with has to do with pre-retirees and retirees who have spent a large portion of their lives saving up money in a defined contribution plan (i.e., 401(k), 403(b), 457, etc.). The amount of these funds can vary widely. I have helped clients who have $50,000 saved up and it was everything they had and needed to protect it. On the other hand, I have had clients whose nest-egg has grown to $5,000,000. Regardless of the amount, protecting those funds and planning for their retirement is critical. So, I would like to look closer at how we use FIAs to accomplish that task.

If you want to accumulate wealth through investments, you can adhere to the golden rule: "The more risk, the more reward." This almost always holds true. If you invest in something that is legitimately guaranteed, like a federal bond, it will only offer a small yield because you are not taking any risk as an investor, so the entity offering it (in this case, the U.S. government) does not have to do much to attract you. In fact, it is the guarantee itself that is attractive, not the return. When is the last time you heard someone say, "Man! I can't wait to purchase some ten-year T-bonds! That 1% return is exciting!"? You will discover that people purchase T-bonds because of their safety and security, which is because the bond is backed by the full faith of the U.S. government.

On the other side of the spectrum, if you invest in something without guarantees, something that can lose value, it should offer a higher return. This is known as *risk premium*, or in other words, there needs to be a premium for the investor to take the risk. The entity looking for the investment in this case needs to offer a higher return to attract the investor because they can't attract them with guarantees. Examples of these types of investments could be startup companies, hedge funds, private equity funds, and speculative investments. The Securities and Exchange Commission (SEC) oversees a broad array of these investments, and an investor can find whatever they are looking for, from conservative bonds to insanely risky stocks.

Looking at the following graphic, you'll see that investments like federal bonds, CDs (certificates of deposit), and money market accounts are considered very safe, but will yield very little. On the other side of the spectrum, individual stocks, junk bonds, and precious metals have much more volatility and risk but can yield a higher payday. Fixed indexed annuities are a hybrid product that are primarily built from blocks on the foundation of the pyramid (high-grade corporate bonds being the largest contributor), but also have some allocation into higher risk/reward investments, primarily call options (as discussed in Chapter 4).

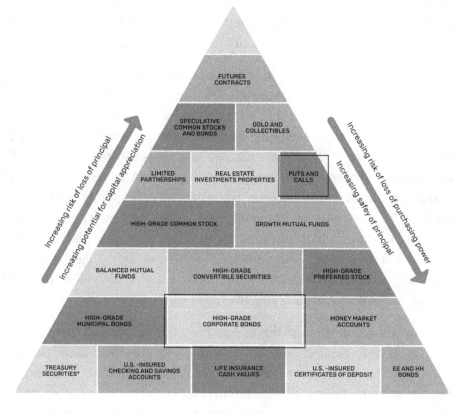

*If held to maturity. Otherwise, they are subject to volatility due to interest rate risk as with any other type of bond.

So, if I were to tell you that you could potentially have the best of both worlds, would you believe it? Probably not, but as you will see, FIAs get you closer to that dream investment than anything else. They have been mathematically proven to outperform bond investments long term, they will average higher returns than CDs and money market accounts, and they offer sound financial security and guarantees to the investor, like a bank product or U.S. Treasury

Bond. On the flip side, will they outperform stocks? I think the best way to answer that is, "not usually." See, FIAs *participate* in market returns; therefore, by design, they can't *beat* the market. If the market does have a sequence with downturns, the FIA's immunity to losing money can create periods where it outperforms the stock market. However, purchasing FIAs to beat the market is foolish. They are there to provide safe accumulation that is superior to bonds and CDs while adding the seven benefits for flexibility and agility in conquering the many retirement challenges.

In 2018, Roger Ibbotson, a finance professor from Yale, wrote an article titled "Fixed Indexed Annuities Beat Out Bonds." In this article, he released his study that shows the back tested performance of stocks, bonds, and FIAs from 1927 to 2016. Let's first look at the maximum annualized three-year return on FIAs vs. stocks and compare it to bonds vs. stocks. With FIAs, the maximum annualized three-year return was 27.56%, whereas stocks were 30.76%. When we compare that to bonds, we see that the maximum annualized three-year return for them was just 23.30%, which is 4.26% lower than FIAs. If someone said, "Hey, do you want a guaranteed investment in retirement that offers X, or X + 4.26%?" Which one would you take?

Now, on the other side of the equation is the safety and guarantee. Like I said before, if you want a secure investment, you can't expect much return, yet we see that FIAs offer a very competitive three-year maximum return compared to stocks, and one that is over 18% higher than that of bonds. When we look at the guarantee and safety from market loss, the FIA historically outperforms both.

When Ibbotson reports the minimum (or worst) three-year annualized return for stocks, he reports a loss of -27.00%. This makes sense because we know that stocks have risk. When we look at the same minimum three-year annualized return for FIAs, we see that it is 0.00%. That's right! Zero loss is the worst that the FIA performed. So even though the stocks outperformed FIAs in their best three-year run by approximately 3%, FIAs outperformed stocks by a whopping 27% when it comes to the three worst years—all of this while outperforming bonds by 18.2%.

FIA HYPOTHETICAL NET RETURN (1927 - 2016)

	Large Cap Stocks	Long Term Gov't Bonds	FIA
Annualized Return	9.92%	5.32%	5.81%
Standard Deviation	19.99%	9.97%	10.01%
Minimum Annualized 3 - Year Return	-27.00%	-2.32%	0.00%
Maximum Annualized 3 - Year Return	30.76%	23.30%	27.56%

Sources: 2017 SBBI Yearbook, Roger G. Ibbotson, Duff & Phelps: Zebra Capital; AnnGen Development, LLC

As I stated earlier, there is always a catch, and I will cover that in Chapter 9, but when it comes to benefits versus drawbacks (limited liquidity and surrender charges), FIAs fit perfectly for most safe money accumulation scenarios.

FIAs for Income

Annuities are commonly known for their ability to pay an annuitant for life. That has been the hallmark of annuities in the United States for over 100 years. As we have discussed, this is a unique and distinct advantage that an annuity or life insurance company can offer, but what *type* of annuity you use and *how* you take lifetime income are choices you can make. We examine those three options next:

> **Annuitization:** The term *annuitization* refers to turning a lump sum into lifetime payments. These payments can be for an individual life or a certain period of time, like ten, twenty, or twenty-five years, or both. When I say both, I mean the longer of the two. For example, if I have

$100,000 that I annuitize on a 65-year-old man, it might pay somewhere around $6,000 per year. This calculation is based on an estimated return on the $100,000 that the annuity company can gain (this return can be higher or lower based on current market conditions, primarily the prevailing yields of bond investments). It is also calculating the expected lifespan of the 65-year-old male, or mortality risk factor.

Remember, mortality credits are very critical and unique for insurance products, including annuities. Mortality credits are simply the amount of additional payment beyond the principal and the interest earned, and it is based on how old the annuitant is. So, if a 65-year-old male annuitized $100,000 and received $6,000 per year for the rest of his life, that $6,000 payment would be mostly a return of his principal and some interest return, and the remainder would be the mortality credit. The older an annuitant is, the more mortality credits they get, and therefore the larger payment they get.

If we have a 70-year-old male and a 65-year-old male and they both "annuitize" $100,000, they are both putting in the same premium and they are both entitled to the same interest. However, the 70-year-old male would receive somewhere around $6,920 per year, which is $920 more, or 15.3% higher, than the 65-year-old male. Why is this? That is the power of mortality credits. If the average male is going to live to 85 years old, then the annuitant who is 70 years old is closer to that age of death, and therefore will get higher allocations of mortality credits to speed up his return. The younger annuitant will get smaller allocations of mortality credits but will receive them for a longer period of time, based on mortality risk.

The graphic below illustrates mortality credits as an additional amount of monthly income with respect to return of principal and interest. Under normal circumstances, a 65-year-old female with $250,000 might traditionally apply the 4% safe withdrawal rule and pay herself $833 per month. With the addition of mortality credits, she can now receive 5.8% or $1212 per month for life. This is an additional $379 per month or a 45% increase that is guaranteed for life. This is why annuities have always been the undisputed champion when it comes to guaranteed lifetime income.

THE BREAKDOWN OF A 65 FEMALE ANNUITY PAYMENT FOR $ 1,212 PER MONTH

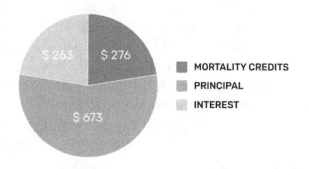

As powerful as annuitization is, there is one drawback. When you annuitize, you surrender all your principal for lifetime payments. Even though you are essentially creating a pension, the psychological effect of "giving up your principal" makes this decision difficult for many. This is understandable, because a guaranteed lifetime income stream is great, but not if you have an emergency and can't access your principal. Another reason some consumers don't like annuitization is because they have an ignorant or antiquated understanding of how the contracts are setup. Many of today's retirees believe that annuitization is a gamble. If you live a long time, it will pay off, but if you die too early, you will not even receive the amount of principal that you put into the annuity.

This is simply not true. Most annuities today that are annuitized will have a guaranteed period of payments or a minimum guaranteed return of principle. This means that if you annuitize your money with the idea that you will live for twenty-five years but you die after ten years, your beneficiaries will get the remainder of payments or principal. Either way, you avoid the "losing bet."

An example of guaranteed payments is something called *period certain* annuitization. With this form of annuitization, an annuitant can select a guaranteed lifetime payout option, but can add a period certain years for guaranteed payout, even if the annuitant dies earlier than expected. The number of years can range from five all the way up to twenty five. So, if Jane paid in $100,000 of premium into a lifetime annuity at age 65 and her annual payment was $5,800, but she elected to have the annuity pay her for a period certain of twenty years, then even if she were to die at age 75, when she had only received $58,000 of her original principle, her beneficiary would receive ten more years of payments, or another $58,000.

Return of principle is a similar protection, but functions as a lump sum upon death. Using the example above, if Jane died unexpectedly at age 75 and had only been paid out $58,000 of her original $100,000, then her beneficiary would receive a single payment for the difference, or $42,000.

Keep in mind that both examples above are descriptive illustrations of how the features work. Many variations of these features can be found, and interest rates are constantly changing, so consult your financial professional and choose the right one for you.

Guaranteed Withdrawal (Income Riders): A more recent form of lifetime income is through something called an *income rider*. This rider is simply an appendix to your annuity agreement that guarantees the annuitant a lifetime annual withdrawal amount that, even if they live so long that the principal is exhausted and the annuity has no more funds, the annuity company will continue to pay them the contracted amount until the annuitant dies.

This type of rider was originally developed to be added on to variable annuities but is also very common with FIAs. Consumers often prefer this form of lifetime income because, even though it will give a slightly lower guaranteed payment compared to annuitization, it still allows access to their principal in case of emergencies.

It is important to note that the annuitization method and the income rider method also have different tax ramifications. Annuitization has the additional benefit of something called an *exclusion ratio*, which makes up a very small part of every annuity payment and is not taxed. However, for most retirees, those with a few hundred thousand dollars, not tens of millions of dollars in retirement, the exclusion ratio is too small to make a substantial difference.

SWIF: There is a third method of income from FIAs that closely mirrors that used with modern portfolio theory: *systematic withdrawal income funding* (SWIF).

Just as the name states, SWIF is a method of creating income through systematic withdrawals. The system used can vary; it could be a fixed percentage, it could be a rising or declining percentage, or it could simply be the interest earned that crediting period. Let me give examples of each of these.

Remember, inside an FIA, you have established that you can't be credited a negative number. The worst you can do is receive a zero, or no interest crediting when the index declines. Most financial planning is done with historical averages, something called *back casting*. An example of historical average of an index performance closely mirrors that used with modern portfolio theory. You can see that this "back casted" number is 6.08%, which is the average annual rate of return (more accurately, the geometric mean return) inside the annuity over the past ten years.

CONTRACT YEAR	ASSUMED INTEREST RATE	ACCUMULATED VALUE
1	0.00%	$ 105,00
2	10.35%	$ 115,870
3	7.14%	$ 124,144
4	0.00%	$ 124,144
5	10.10%	$ 136,677
6	14.09%	$ 155,931
7	5.78%	$ 164,936
8	0.00%	$ 164,936
9	0.00%	$ 164,936
10	14.97%	$ 189,631

Product Geometric Mean Interest Rate = 6.08%

As you can see, the index never actually hit 6.08% in any one given year. In fact, it had four years (years 1, 4, 8, and 9) that it was credited 0%, which is far better than losing money in those years, but if you total all credits together and divide the total by the total number of years, you get the average, which is 6.24%. (the geometric mean, which is shown here, will vary slightly from the average because it considers the sequence and compounding effect of the returns, but for this illustration they are close enough)

Now that we have established an average, we can choose a percentage that we want to take each year. Let's say 5%. Based on the previous ten-year performance, we can assume that there will be years where the 5% will be coming out of the interest that we have earned and there will be years where it will be coming out of our principal, and in some instances both. But knowing that we cannot get less than zero, and knowing that our average was 6.08%, we can create a plan that most would consider stable through 5% withdrawals rather than annuitization or an income rider. An illustration of this is shown below.

YEAR ENDING	BEGINNING OF YEAR AGE	END OF YEAR AGE	FREE PARTIAL WITHDRAWALS	CUMULATIVE WITHDRAWALS	ACCUMULATED VALUE
11/2019	65	66	$ 0	$ 0	$ 111,394
11/2020	66	67	$ 5,570	$ 5,570	$ 112,268
11/2021	67	68	$ 5,613	$ 11,183	$ 113,150
11/2022	68	69	$ 5,657	$ 16,841	$ 114,038
11/2023	69	70	$ 5,702	$ 22,542	$ 114,933
11/2024	70	71	$ 5,747	$ 28,289	$ 115,835
11/2025	71	72	$ 5,792	$ 34,081	$ 116,744
11/2026	72	73	$ 5,837	$ 39,918	$ 117,661
11/2027	73	74	$ 5,883	$ 45,801	$ 118,584
11/2028	74	75	$ 5,929	$ 51,730	$ 119,515
11/2029	75	76	$ 5,976	$ 57,706	$ 120,453

And if we ran the same scenario against the actual ten-year returns, not the average, it would look like this:

YEAR ENDING	BEGINNING OF YEAR AGE	END OF YEAR AGE	ANNUAL ASSUMED INTEREST RATE	FREE PARTIAL WITHDRAWALS	CUMULATIVE WITHDRAWALS	ACCUMULATED VALUE
11/2019	65	66	0.00%	$ 0	$ 0	$ 105,000
11/2020	66	67	10.35%	$ 5,250	$ 5,250	$ 110,077
11/2021	67	68	7.14%	$ 5,504	$ 10,754	$ 112,040
11/2022	68	69	0.00%	$ 5,602	$ 16,356	$ 106,438
11/2023	69	70	10.10%	$ 5,322	$ 21,678	$ 111,324
11/2024	70	71	14.09%	$ 5,566	$ 27,244	$ 120,656
11/2025	71	72	5.78%	$ 6,033	$ 33,277	$ 121,243
11/2026	72	73	0.00%	$ 6,062	$ 39,339	$ 115,181
11/2027	73	74	0.00%	$ 5,759	$ 45,098	$ 109,422
11/2028	74	75	14.97%	$ 5,471	$ 50,569	$ 119,515
11/2029	75	76	0.00%	$ 5,976	$ 56,545	$ 113,539

In both scenarios, the client was able to take out 5% and still have more money than they started with. Although there is no guarantee or way to predict how much your exact crediting will be, it is far more reliable, stable, and less scary doing interest withdrawals from a vehicle that can't credit a negative value versus a volatile market that can lose value. This percentage can change each year, and it could be an increasing number (say for older or less healthy clients) or it could be smaller, perhaps reflecting a slowdown with age in retirement spending. How one wants to customize their SWIF approach based on their unique circumstances is up to them, but a good rule of thumb is to stay below the back casted average rate of return.

The last example of SWIF would be the interest-only withdrawal scenario. With this method, the client takes out the interest (limited by the amount permitted by the annuity's surrender charge and market value adjustment or MVA, which I will explain more in Chapter 9) as income and leaves the remaining principal or principal and remaining interest intact. Conversely, in years where the index does not return any interest, the client will not take withdrawals.

YEAR ENDING	BEGINNING OF YEAR AGE	END OF YEAR AGE	ANNUAL ASSUMED INTEREST RATE	FREE PARTIAL WITHDRAWALS	CUMULATIVE WITHDRAWALS	ACCUMULATED VALUE
11/2019	65	66	0.00%	$ 0	$ 0	$ 100,000
11/2020	66	67	11.39%	$ 0	$ 0	$ 111,388
11/2021	67	68	7.85%	$ 11,139	$ 11,139	$ 108,123
11/2022	68	69	0.00%	$ 7,874	$ 19,013	$ 100,249
11/2023	69	70	11.11%	$ 0	$ 19,013	$ 111,382
11/2024	70	71	15.50%	$ 11,133	$ 30,146	$ 115,783
11/2025	71	72	6.35%	$ 11,578	$ 41,724	$ 110,825
11/2026	72	73	0.00%	$ 6,620	$ 48,344	$ 104,205
11/2027	73	74	0.00%	$ 0	$ 48,344	$ 104,205
11/2028	74	75	16.47%	$ 0	$ 48,344	$ 121,367
11/2029	75	76	0.00%	$ 17,162	$ 65,506	$ 104,205

In all three SWIF scenarios, you can see that the cumulative withdrawals and value at the end of ten years were roughly the same. This is a function of stability with withdrawal methods forged using the FIA, which is a tool that does not allow for negative crediting.

Annuity Taxation

As we have learned, annuities grow tax deferred. We have also just learned about two ways that annuity funds can be accessed, annuitization or withdrawals, so let's discuss how annuity funds are taxed in both of these situations.

When we are dealing with true annuitization, we are taxed in a "blended" method, where each annuity payment is a combination of interest and mortality crediting (which is taxed as ordinary income), return of principal (not taxed), and the small portion of the payment we discussed earlier that is not interest or principal, called the exclusion ratio (which is also not taxed). Curtis Cloke is credited with the trademarked term "F.I.B.O." which stands for *First In Blended Out* and represents the unique way that annuitization payments are treated by the IRS (more information about Curtis Cloke and his retirement income solutions can be found at www.curtiscloke.com). True annuitization (payments where you can never access your principal again) are the most favorable to an annuitant when it comes to tax treatment, but as stated earlier, many retirees don't like the idea of losing access to their principle for emergencies or changes in expenses.

When withdrawals are made from an annuity, the tax is based on the L.I.F.O. taxation system. That is *Last In First Out*, which means the last funds put into the annuity will be the first to be taken out. With an annuity, the principle was placed in first, and the interest is placed in last. So, the interest will be the first to be withdrawn and is taxed as ordinary income.

For example, if John Doe placed $100,000 of principle into an annuity seven years ago, and the annuity has grown to $150,000, it represents $100,000 of principle and $50,000 of interest. If John then withdraws $30,000, he will be taxed as ordinary income levels for the $30,000 because the interest is taken out first. If he were to take out $75,000, then the first $50,000 would be taxed as ordinary income and the last $25,000 would not be taxed because it would be considered a return of principle. Remember, if any annuity is an IRA (individual retirement account), then all withdrawals are taxed regardless of the method used (i.e., annuitization or withdrawal).

Now, we look at some real-world solution where FIAs have been used to solve some client challenges. The following scenarios are real and represent actual clients I've encountered and helped with FIAs. For the protection of their identities, I've changed their names, but their solutions are very real and will resonate with millions of other Americans today and in the future.

Ken and Anne – Solving the Income Gap

Ken is 64 and in average health. He currently takes cholesterol and high blood pressure medicine and is about twenty pounds overweight. He has a history of heart disease in his family and his father and grandfather both died before they turned 80. Ken plans on retiring next year. Anne is four years younger than Ken (she is 60) and is in great health. She exercises regularly, takes no doctor prescribed medication, and her parents and grandparents both lived into their 90s.

When I met with them, Ken was in the twilight of his successful career as a sales representative for a nationwide distributor. Anne had worked for several years as a substitute teacher but had not been employed for the past five years, and she also had a nine-year period where she was not working while raising their two children. As a result, her Social Security income is scheduled to be less than half of what Ken's will be when she is eligible.

Their primary concern is having enough money for Anne later in life when Ken dies. They know they can best prepare for this by delaying Ken's Social Security until age 70 and creating some sort of guaranteed income stream that passes onto Anne, but they aren't sure how to best accomplish this. Their assets and Social Security amounts are listed below.

The first challenge is allowing Ken to retire at 65 while delaying his Social Security to 70. Remember, when Ken dies (let's say he passes at 80), Anne, who would only be 76, would lose the lower of the two Social Security payments. Allowing the higher of the two Social Security payments (Ken's) to pass on and continue to grow with CPI puts Anne in the best place for a fruitful retirement after Ken's death.

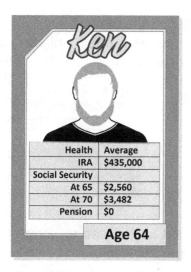

Health	Average
IRA	$435,000
Social Security	
At 65	$2,560
At 70	$3,482
Pension	$0

Age 64

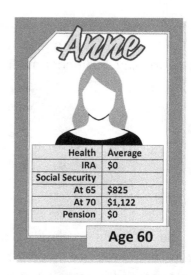

Health	Average
IRA	$0
Social Security	
At 65	$825
At 70	$1,122
Pension	$0

Age 60

We first calculated how much they would need monthly for the next five years without claiming Social Security. We also decided that Ken would work part-time, something he had not considered previously. As it turns out, he was able to stay on part-time as a consultant for his previous company, which allowed him to make $24,000 a year. They calculated that they would only need an additional $20,000 more per year to have enough to pay their bills and allow them to defer Ken's Social Security until age 70. Here is how we planned to solve the problem using an FIA to help.

We deposited $250,000 of Ken's IRA into an FIA. From age 64 to 70, Ken will withdraw $20,000 a year to supplement his income and delay his Social Security to age 70.

BEGINNING OF YEAR AGE (ANNUITANT/SPOUSE)	END OF YEAR AGE (ANNUITANT/SPOUSE)	FREE PARTIAL WITHDRAWALS	RMD WITHDRAWALS	LIFETIME INCOME WITHDRAWALS	CUMULATIVE WITHDRAWALS	BENEFIT BASE	ACCUMULATED VALUE	CASH SURRENDER VALUE	DEATH BENEFIT
64/60	65/61	$20,000	$0	$0	$20,000	$284,567	$234,667	$215,997	$234,667
65/61	66/62	$20,000	$0	$0	$40,000	$286,767	$229,737	$209,737	$229,986
66/62	67/63	$20,000	$0	$0	$60,000	$269,206	$214,207	$197,470	$214,207
67/63	68/64	$20,000	$0	$0	$80,000	$268,424	$208,123	$193,904	$208,123
68/64	69/65	$20,000	$0	$0	$100,000	$249,384	$191,868	$180,656	$191,868
69/65	70/66	$20,000	$0	$0	$120,000	$244,850	$184,235	$175,275	$184,235

From age 71 through 80, Ken allows the FIA to grow and build up income for later in life. RMDs are taken from the other $185,000 that we did not place into the FIA, which will help maximize the amount of lifetime income drawn from the FIA once it is activated.

At age 80, we predict Ken activating the guaranteed, joint lifetime income rider and using the money to help offset inflation and prepare for any additional medical costs Ken will incur in his 80s.

80/76	81/77	$0	$0	$23,896	$143,896	$400,010	$269,222	$269,222	$269,222
81/77	82/78	$0	$0	$24,345	$168,241	$395,432	$262,931	$262,931	$262,931
82/78	83/79	$0	$0	$26,139	$194,380	$363,818	$241,190	$241,190	$241,190
83/79	84/80	$0	$0	$26,625	$221,005	$381,449	$230,447	$230,447	$230,447
84/80	85/81	$0	$0	$28,596	$249,601	$314,333	$205,562	$205,562	$205,562
85/81	86/82	$0	$0	$29,122	$276,723	$292,748	$189,552	$189,552	$189,552
86/82	87/83	$0	$0	$31,286	$310,008	$249,470	$161,147	$161,147	$161,147

87/83	88/84	$0	$0	$31,855	$341,863	$217,036	$138,938	$138,938	$138,938
88/84	89/85	$0	$0	$34,232	$376,095	$166,863	$106,592	$106,592	$106,592
89/85	90/86	$0	$0	$34,848	$410,943	$101,714	$77,118	$77,118	$72,118
90/86	91/87	$0	$0	$37,458	$448,401	$63,813	$40,366	$40,366	$40,366
91/87	92/88	$0	$0	$38,126	$486,526	$3,838	$2,409	$2,409	$2,409
92/88	93/89	$0	$0	$40,992	$527,519	$0	$0	$0	$0
93/89	94/90	$0	$0	$41,624	$569,342	$0	$0	$0	$0
94/90	95/91	$0	$0	$44,635	$614,177	$0	$0	$0	$0

Regardless of when Ken dies, or when he decides to activate the joint income rider, the income from the FIA continues to both flow in for Anne and indexes upwards each year that the market grows, even after Ken's death. If Anne dies at age 90, then they would have converted $250,000 into $614,177 *while* withdrawing money from it day one and at an average assumed rate of return of just 4.56%. Keep in mind that if Anne lived to 100 or beyond, she would still receive these increasing payments, and if she died earlier than expected, she would pass on a death benefit to their children.

Susan – Maximizing Social Security

Susan is single, 54 years old, and in excellent health. After meeting her, I learned that she wants to retire at age 63 but understands the value of delaying Social Security until age 67 (her FRA) because of her high likelihood of longevity. She came to me through a referral when she inherited $200,000 from an older uncle who had passed at age 90. She is still contributing to her 403(b) at the hospital where she works. Her 403(b) is currently at $288,000 and her employer offers a 3% match to contributions. She wants to retire in her early 60s so she can take time and travel the world while she is still young enough to enjoy it.

Susan's first challenge is figuring out a way to bridge her income from the end of her employment to the beginning of her Social Security payments, which is approximately four years. Her second challenge is allocating additional money during this time to support her travel desires. Finally, she needs to create a plan to ensure she does not run out of money in retirement, which is a sincere concern because of her great health and her family's history of longevity.

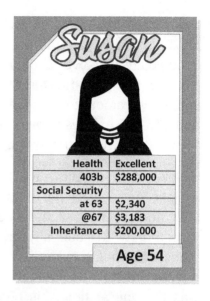

Health	Excellent
403b	$288,000
Social Security	
at 63	$2,340
@67	$3,183
Inheritance	$200,000

Age 54

The first advice I gave Susan was for her to continue to make her 403(b) contributions up to the employer match of 3% for the remainder of her time working, which is approximately nine years. A rule in investing is to always take free money when you can get it, and an employer match on your defined contribution plan is exactly that—free money! Her investment selections in her 403(b) were relatively conservative, so we felt good about the account not declining in value over the long run, with the intention of selecting even more conservative investment options as she approached age 60.

Next, we decide to put the $200,000 into a fixed indexed annuity that would allow her non-qualified inheritance to grow tax deferred and eliminate all fees and market loss. She made this decision because she knew she wanted to see higher earning potential than investment grade bonds or CDs could provide, but she didn't want to worry about participating in losses if the market did decline over the next nine years leading up to retirement. In addition to that, the FIA we chose provided a 9% ($18,000) upfront premium bonus to her account value, which brought her interest-yielding premium to $218,000. This FIA allows for flexible spending to meet her goals while ensuring she won't lose money to fees or market loss.

Utilizing an FIA that was built for accumulation and had averaged 6.02% per year over the previous ten years, Susan is projected to accumulate just over $400,000 by age 63. She can then withdraw $75,000 per year for three years from the annuity. This annual withdrawal amount comprises $60,000 to cover her living expenses and $15,000 to cover travel expenses. We have made assumptions for taxation within these figures.

Following three years of $75,000 withdrawals, she is now eligible to take out $3,183 per month of Social Security benefits (which will grow each year there is a CPI-W increase). She continues to withdraw $10,000 a year from the FIA to cover her traveling costs and does this until she reaches age 72. At this time, she is required to take her required minimum distributions (age 72 RMD was the age at time this book was written), and she can choose to withdraw RMDs from the FIA or take them out of her 403(b) (which would have been converted to an IRA at this point, and is also going to be substantially higher than the $288,000 when I first met her), or she can take out some from both the FIA and her IRA. Either way, her careful planning and leverage of FIAs has allowed her the ability to accomplish her retirement goals while keeping her savings safe from fees and market downturns.

Beginning of Year Age	End of Year Age	Free Partial Withdrawals	Cumulative Withdrawals	Accumulated Value	Cash Surrender Value[1]	Death Benefit
52	53	$0	$0	$205,674	$188,963	$205,674
53	54	$0	$0	$224,794	$206,822	$224,794
54	55	$0	$0	$231,130	$214,647	$231,130
55	56	$0	$0	$252,672	$236,832	$252,672
56	57	$0	$0	$259,747	$245,913	$259,747
57	58	$0	$0	$284,019	$271,117	$284,019
58	59	$0	$0	$291,920	$281,379	$291,920
59	60	$0	$0	$319,269	$319,269	$319,269
60	61	$0	$0	$328,092	$328,092	$328,092
61	62	$0	$0	$358,908	$358,908	$358,908
62	63	$0	$0	$368,761	$368,761	$368,761
63	64	$0	$0	$403,486	$403,486	$403,486
64	65	$75,000	$75,000	$337,443	$337,443	$337,443
65	66	$75,000	$150,000	$287,220	$287,220	$287,220
66	67	$75,000	$225,000	$217,968	$217,968	$217,968
67	68	$10,000	$235,000	$227,652	$227,652	$227,652
68	69	$10,000	$245,000	$223,507	$223,507	$223,507
69	70	$10,000	$255,000	$233,767	$233,767	$233,767
70	71	$10,000	$265,000	$229,746	$229,746	$229,746
71	72	$10,000	$275,000	$240,650	$240,650	$240,650
72	73	$0	$275,000	$247,037	$247,037	$247,037
73	74	$0	$275,000	$270,596	$270,596	$270,596
74	75	$0	$275,000	$277,728	$277,728	$277,728
75	76	$0	$275,000	$304,282	$304,282	$304,282
76	77	$0	$275,000	$312,245	$312,245	$312,245
77	78	$0	$275,000	$342,175	$342,175	$342,175
78	79	$25,000	$300,000	$325,418	$325,418	$325,418
79	80	$0	$300,000	$356,688	$356,688	$356,688
80	81	$0	$300,000	$365,893	$365,893	$365,893

Around age 78, she plans on needing to replace her car, so she will again withdraw from their FIA to find a car within her budget. Following that, she knows that she will want to help pay for her only granddaughter's college or another charitable gift, so we project a $50,000 donation in her mid-80s, and finally, we project $100,000 per year to help her with long-term care and end-of-life expenses in her 90s. With all this, she still is projected to have over $300,000 by age 95, which bolsters her position and ability to conquer these retirement challenges as they come, while making enjoyment of retirement a priority.

Beginning of Year Age	End of Year Age	Free Partial Withdrawals	Cumulative Withdrawals	Accumulated Value	Cash Surrender Value[1]	Death Benefit
81	82	$0	$300,000	$401,140	$401,140	$401,140
82	83	$0	$300,000	$411,420	$411,420	$411,420
83	84	$0	$300,000	$451,151	$451,151	$451,151
84	85	$0	$300,000	$462,630	$462,630	$462,630
85	86	$50,000	$350,000	$452,578	$452,578	$452,578
86	87	$0	$350,000	$464,011	$464,011	$464,011
87	88	$0	$350,000	$509,044	$509,044	$509,044
88	89	$0	$350,000	$521,811	$521,811	$521,811
89	90	$0	$350,000	$572,578	$572,578	$572,578
90	91	$100,000	$450,000	$484,346	$484,346	$484,346
91	92	$100,000	$550,000	$421,830	$421,830	$421,830
92	93	$100,000	$650,000	$329,786	$329,786	$329,786
93	94	$0	$650,000	$362,028	$362,028	$362,028
94	95	$0	$650,000	$370,912	$370,912	$370,912

This scenario is where FIAs shine. By eliminating fees and market risk, and allowing non-qualified money to grow tax deferred, we can leverage the FIA and increase the potency of the client's Social Security and defined contribution plan, which optimizes her retirement.

Joe and Dominique – Leaving A Legacy

Joe and Dominique want to leave money to their grandchildren for college, but they want to be prepared for potential long-term care overrun costs and income shortfall. Joe is 67 and Dominique is 66, and they are both in average health. They have saved up a combined $385,000 in their IRAs, and Joe has a pension of which 50% passes onto Dominique when he dies. Both were already collecting Social Security benefits when I met them. Joe's Social Security payment is $2080 a month and Dominique's is $1125 per month.

As stated, their primary concern is helping their three grandchildren pay for college, but they are realistic in understanding that they must ensure they have a secure retirement first, especially if Joe passes first and Dominique loses both the lesser of the two Social Security payments and half of Joe's pension. When I first met them, they had not started accessing their combined IRA accounts.

I explained to Joe and Dominique that they have done a great job in preparing for retirement. They have saved nearly $400,000 between them, were entitled to a relatively large pension, and had both contributed to and were now collecting Social Security income. Furthermore, they had done a great job controlling their expenses. They had very few bills and their home and vehicles were paid off.

Health	Average
403b	$205,000
Social Security	$2,080
Pension	$2,800

Age 67

Health	Average
IRA	$180,000
Social Security	$1,125
Pension	$1,400*
* upon Joe's Death	

Age 66

We decided to utilize two different FIAs to accomplish our goals, and both FIAs offered flexibility to account for any future changes in the retirement plan. First, we used a unique FIA that was built for accumulation and included a death benefit rider that for 0.30% per year, a 30% bonus is added to the account value when the annuitant dies. This FIA had performed well historically, with its worst ten-year period of performance averaging returns over 7%, and the average annual returns over the past ten years over 9%

	Last 10 Years 1/1/2010 – 12/31/2019			Lowest 10-Year Period 1/1/2002 – 12/31/2011			Highest 10-Year Period 1/1/2010 – 12/31/2019		
Contract Year	Index Rate	Interest Credited	Accumulation Value	Index Rate	Interest Credited	Accumulation Value	Index Rate	Interest Credited	Accumulation Value
1	3.06%	$2,250	$75,713	0.00%	$0	$73,463	3.06%	$2,250	$75,713
2	3.06%	$2,250	$76,410	3.06%	$2,250	$74,207	3.06%	$2,250	$76,410
3	3.06%	$2,250	$77,094	3.06%	$2,250	$74,935	3.06%	$2,250	$77,094
4	3.06%	$2,250	$77,764	3.06%	$2,250	$75,649	3.06%	$2,250	$77,764
5	72.16%	$52,972	$129,141	38.03%	$27,930	$102,028	72.16%	$52,972	$129,141
6	3.06%	$3,874	$130,368	3.06%	$3,061	$102,997	3.06%	$3,874	$130,368
7	3.06%	$3,874	$131,570	3.06%	$3,061	$103,947	3.06%	$3,874	$131,570
8	3.06%	$3,874	$132,747	3.06%	$3,061	$104,877	3.06%	$3,874	$132,747
9	3.06%	$3,874	$133,900	3.06%	$3,061	$105,788	3.06%	$3,874	$133,900
10	41.20%	$52,071	$183,225	46.31%	$46,241	$149,860	41.20%	$52,071	$183,225
	Average Annualized Return = 9.34%			Average Annualized Return = 7.17%			Average Annualized Return = 9.34%		

Legend:
- Last 10 Years
- Lowest
- Highest

Assumes a new contract is issued at the start of each 10-year calendar year period over the past 20 years at the current index crediting rate and held for 10 years with no withdrawals. The highest and lowest dates are based on the highest and lowest 10-year index returns.

The True Up provision may positively affect the Accumulation Value in the 10-year period scenarios.

We elected to fund this annuity with $75,000 of Dominique's IRA. Although they can take out up to 10% a year of this annuity without any penalty, they plan on taking out required minimum distributions (RMDs) once Dominique turns age 72. If we hypothetically guess that Dominique dies at age 86, then they would have withdrawn $105,811 dollars in RMDs, and have a remaining FIA balance of $212,481. Because of the unique death benefit rider found on this FIA, the $212,481 balance at the time of Dominique's death would receive an extra 30% crediting, which would make the total death benefit passed on to her beneficiaries a whopping $276,225. Just in case Joe is still alive when Dominique passes, we made Joe the primary beneficiary, but assuming Joe would most likely not be alive, at the time of Dominiques death, we made the three grandchildren as contingent beneficiaries, with a third ownership each. This would give each grandchild an estimated $90,000 for college and the amount would pass free of probate or could even fund a trust with clear guidelines on how the money should be spent on behalf of the grandchildren.

This serves as a powerful example of how proper planning and use of an FIA can help in achieving your retirement goals with just a portion of your retirement savings (in this case, $75,000). This

End of Year	Age	Premium	Withdrawal or RMD	Optimizer Fee	Rider Fee	Credited Rate	Interest Credited	Accumulation Value	Cash Surrender Value	Guaranteed Minimum Value	Enhanced Death Benefit*
1	67	$75,000	$0	$1,313	$225	3.06%	$2,250	$75,713	$66,627	$66,660	$75,713
2	68	$0	$0	$1,325	$227	3.06%	$2,250	$76,410	$68,494	$68,580	$76,410
3	69	$0	$0	$1,337	$229	3.06%	$2,250	$77,094	$69,454	$69,614	$77,094
4	70	$0	$0	$1,349	$231	3.06%	$2,250	$77,764	$70,408	$70,662	$101,093
5	71	$0	$0	$1,361	$233	72.16%	$52,972	$129,141**	$117,005	$71,724	$167,883
6	72	$0	$0	$2,260	$387	3.06%	$3,874	$130,368	$119,797	$73,158	$169,478
7	73	$0	$5,093	$2,192	$376	3.06%	$3,721	$126,428	$117,357	$69,882	$164,357
8	74	$0	$5,119	$2,123	$364	3.06%	$3,568	$122,390	$114,708	$66,416	$159,107
9	75	$0	$5,143	$2,052	$352	3.06%	$3,414	$118,257	$111,896	$62,806	$153,734
10	76	$0	$5,165	$1,979	$339	41.20%	$43,797	$154,571	$147,433	$59,051	$200,942
11	77	$0	$7,026	$2,582	$443	3.06%	$4,426	$148,946	$148,946	$55,332	$193,630
12	78	$0	$7,026	$2,484	$426	3.06%	$4,216	$143,227	$143,227	$48,789	$186,195
13	79	$0	$7,056	$2,383	$409	3.06%	$4,004	$137,383	$137,383	$42,150	$178,598
14	80	$0	$7,046	$2,281	$391	3.06%	$3,793	$131,458	$131,458	$35,455	$170,895
15	81	$0	$7,030	$2,177	$373	72.17%	$84,321	$206,198	$206,198	$28,709	$268,058
16	82	$0	$11,520	$3,407	$584	3.06%	$5,840	$196,528	$196,528	$17,361	$255,486
17	83	$0	$11,493	$3,238	$555	3.06%	$5,496	$186,737	$186,737	$5,927	$242,758
18	84	$0	$11,457	$3,067	$526	3.06%	$5,152	$176,839	$176,839	$0	$229,890
19	85	$0	$11,409	$2,895	$496	3.06%	$4,810	$166,848	$166,848	$0	$216,902
20	86	$0	$11,274	$2,723	$467	41.20%	$60,096	$212,481	$212,481	$0	$276,225
21	87	$0	$15,070	$3,455	$592	3.06%	$5,922	$199,286	$199,286	$0	$259,072
22	88	$0	$14,873	$3,227	$553	3.06%	$5,476	$186,109	$186,109	$0	$241,942
23	89	$0	$14,655	$3,000	$514	3.06%	$5,036	$172,976	$172,976	$0	$224,868
24	90	$0	$14,415	$2,775	$476	3.06%	$4,604	$159,914	$159,914	$0	$207,888

plan also has flexibility because if they had needed the money or changed their mind about paying for their grandchildren's college, they would have complete access to the funds and ability to change the beneficiaries or redirect the asset.

The second issue we needed to resolve for Joe and Dominique was their desire to never run out of money. To accomplish this, we allocated Joe's IRA ($205,000) into an FIA with an income rider. This FIA generated an immediate income stream of $905 per month and is guaranteed to pay out for as long as either Joe or Dominique is still alive. As is so often the case, Joe and Dominique elected to use the FIA with an income rider instead of full annuitization because they wanted the option to access their principal in an emergency or if their plans changed. The FIA payment is slightly less than what they could have received with a SPIA, but they wanted the flexibility.

This $905 per month wasn't enough to completely cover the gap in lost pension and Social Security if Joe dies before Dominique, but keep in mind that we still have over $100,000 of Dominique's IRA that we did not touch. By the time Joe does pass, if it were to precede Dominique, this additional qualified money should provide the additional income needed, while still offering maximum flexibility.

Steve – Avoiding Market Downturns

Steve is 55 and has had a very successful career at a major software development company. He is now doing some consulting and plans on working part-time while traveling the world over the next eight years. He has nearly $3,000,000 in his retirement account, and he is a believer in the U.S. stock market. However, Steve worked through the 2001 and 2008 recessions, and now in 2020 is more uncomfortable than ever that another bear market is lurking around the corner.

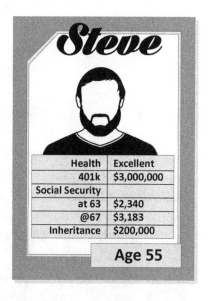

	Steve
Health	Excellent
401k	$3,000,000
Social Security	
at 63	$2,340
@67	$3,183
Inheritance	$200,000

Age 55

Steve wants to set aside enough of his retirement to ensure that he will be able to pay himself $60,000 a year for the rest of his life, no matter what the market does, starting at age 65. He has looked at putting a portion of his retirement into government bonds or CDs, but the low yields would mean that he would have to put away too much of his retirement to reach that target income number. Allocating too much into such conservative investments limits the amount that he can continue to aggressively grow in the market, and any yields or payment streams he receives will not be guaranteed for life.

To accomplish this, we directed $825,000 of his retirement into an A rated FIA carrier with an accumulation annuity that also featured an added on guaranteed lifetime income rider.

This FIA would eliminate all risk from the equation, and even if the market went down every year for the next decade (not likely), he would still receive a guaranteed $60,000 a year starting at age 65 and that would last for the rest of his life.

End Of Year	Age	Purchase Payment	Credited Interest	Lifetime Income Withdrawal	Other Withdrawals	Lifetime Income Rider Charge	Account Value	Surrender Value	Death Benefit
1	55	825,000	0	0	0	7,425	817,575	735,818	817,575
2	56	0	0	0	0	7,358	810,217	744,655	810,217
3	57	0	0	0	0	7,292	802,925	745,173	802,925
4	58	0	0	0	0	7,226	795,699	751,186	795,699
5	59	0	0	0	0	7,161	788,537	758,698	788,537
6	60	0	0	0	0	7,097	781,440	766,285	781,440
7	61	0	0	0	0	7,033	774,407	773,948	774,407
8	62	0	0	0	0	6,970	781,687	781,687	781,687
9	63	0	0	0	0	7,035	789,504	789,504	789,504
10	64	0	0	0	0	7,106	797,399	797,399	797,399
11	65	0	0	60,266	0	6,634	744,504	744,504	744,504

This guarantee, however, is the worst-case scenario. Assuming the markets do perform at an average clip moving forward, we can now recalculate Steve's annuity and see that his guaranteed lifetime income will adjust upward to over $100,000 per year, starting at age 65. So, hypothetically speaking, if he were to activate the income at

End Of Year	Age	Purchase Payment	Credited Interest	Lifetime Income Withdrawal	Other Withdrawals	Lifetime Income Rider Charge	Account Value	Surrender Value	Death Benefit
1	55	825,000	86,378	0	0	8,202	903,175	812,858	903,175
2	56	0	25,650	0	0	8,359	920,466	845,753	920,466
3	57	0	110,548	0	0	9,279	1,021,735	947,360	1,021,735
4	58	0	100,130	0	0	10,097	1,111,768	1,041,096	1,111,768
5	59	0	118,292	0	0	11,071	1,218,989	1,152,521	1,218,989
6	60	0	0	0	0	10,971	1,208,019	1,153,713	1,208,019
7	61	0	131,674	0	0	12,057	1,327,635	1,279,362	1,327,635
8	62	0	131,303	0	0	13,130	1,445,808	1,406,417	1,445,808
9	63	0	0	0	0	13,012	1,432,796	1,407,031	1,432,796
10	64	0	64,906	0	0	13,479	1,484,222	1,470,813	1,484,222
11	65	0	144,333	105,684	0	13,706	1,509,165	1,509,165	1,509,165
12	66	0	39,859	105,684	0	12,990	1,430,349	1,430,349	1,430,349
13	67	0	159,092	105,684	0	13,354	1,470,403	1,470,403	1,470,403
14	68	0	133,742	105,684	0	13,486	1,484,975	1,484,975	1,484,975
15	69	0	146,757	105,684	0	13,734	1,512,313	1,512,313	1,512,313
16	70	0	0	105,684	0	12,660	1,393,969	1,393,969	1,393,969
17	71	0	140,423	105,684	0	12,858	1,415,849	1,415,849	1,415,849
18	72	0	129,575	105,684	0	12,958	1,426,782	1,426,782	1,426,782
19	73	0	0	105,684	0	11,890	1,309,208	1,309,208	1,309,208
20	74	0	54,520	105,684	0	11,322	1,246,721	1,246,721	1,246,721
21	75	0	119,467	105,684	0	11,345	1,249,159	1,249,159	1,249,159
22	76	0	32,475	105,684	0	10,584	1,165,365	1,165,365	1,165,365
23	77	0	127,268	105,684	0	10,683	1,176,266	1,176,266	1,176,266
24	78	0	104,917	105,684	0	10,579	1,164,919	1,164,919	1,164,919
25	79	0	112,703	105,684	0	10,547	1,161,390	1,161,390	1,161,390
26	80	0	0	105,684	0	9,501	1,046,205	1,046,205	1,046,205
27	81	0	102,517	105,684	0	9,387	1,033,650	1,033,650	1,033,650
28	82	0	91,776	105,684	0	9,178	1,010,563	1,010,563	1,010,563
29	83	0	0	105,684	0	8,144	896,735	896,735	896,735
30	84	0	35,835	105,684	0	7,442	819,443	819,443	819,443
31	85	0	74,731	105,684	0	7,096	781,393	781,393	781,393
32	86	0	19,190	105,684	0	6,254	688,645	688,645	688,645
33	87	0	70,014	105,684	0	5,877	647,097	647,097	647,097
34	88	0	53,058	105,684	0	5,350	589,121	589,121	589,121
35	89	0	51,438	105,684	0	4,814	530,060	530,060	530,060

age 65 and live until age 89, he would have now turned his original principal payment of $825,000 into a stream of payments totaling $2,642,100, and still have an account value of $530,060, which he could access as he pleases or have paid as a death benefit to any beneficiary(ies) of his choosing, free of probate.

By allocating a certain percentage of his retirement toward his future guaranteed income needs, Steve has allowed himself to enjoy his retirement worry free and freed up over 72% of his remaining portfolio to spend as he pleases or invest in more aggressive assets that could yield him a larger payout.

Remember, if he did live a very long time, let's say to age 100 or beyond, his annual payment is guaranteed, so he would never have to worry about outliving his money.

CHAPTER VIII

MARKET FRAGILITY — BANKS TO VIRUS

Peaks and Valleys

Everyone knows that the stock market does not go up in a linear line. No, we have peaks and valleys that, over time, trend upward. Partially because of inflation and mostly because of the economic growth of the underlying stocks that comprise the market. As stated earlier, the market goes up more than it goes down, which is why consistent market investment over time is a great way to build wealth. Also, for those who can afford some risk, exposure to the market in retirement can also yield some very handsome returns and tends to fend off inflation challenges.

Most peaks and valleys are simply the result of prevailing market trends and the rising and falling of stock prices relative to the demand and risk appetite. However, some peaks and valleys are initiated by more drastic influences. Let's discuss those.

Let's first look at the historical occurrences of bear markets in the United States. Remember, a bear market represents a sustained loss of 20% or more from the previous high. Just like a bear attack in the wild, these drops are fast, vicious, and can leave your investments devastated, and in some cases, kill your finances altogether! The graphic below lists the history of bear markets experienced in the United States in chronological order

Bear Markets Throughout U.S. History

Start	Length (Mo.)	S&P 500 Change
Sep 1929	32.8	-86.2%
Mar 1937	61.8	-60.00%
May 1946	36.5	-29.6%
Aug 1956	14.7	-21.5%
Dec 1961	6.5	-28.0%
Feb 1966	7.9	-22.2%
Nov 1968	17.8	-36.1%
Jan 1973	20.7	-48.2%
Nov 1980	20.4	-27.1%
Aug 1987	3.3	-33.5%
Jul 1990	2.9	-19.9%
Mar 2000	30.5	-49.1%
Oct 2007	17	-56.8%
Feb 2020	1.1	-33.9%

Source: S&P Global

Now, onto the history of the bull markets. Just the opposite of a bear market, the bull market represents a sustained gain of more

Bull Markets Throughout U.S. History

Start	Length (Mo.)	S&P 500 Change
Jun 1932	57.1	324.5%
Apr 1942	49	157.7%
Jun 1949	85.6	266.3%
Oct 1957	49.7	86.4%
Jun 1962	43.5	79.8%
Oct 1966	25.8	48.0%
May 1970	31.6	73.5%
Oct 1974	73.9	125.6%
Aug 1982	60.4	228.8%
Dec 1987	31.4	64.8%
Oct 1990	113.4	417.0%
Oct 2002	60	101.5%
Mar 2009	131.4	400.5%
Mar 2020	4.9	51.0%

Source: S&P Global

than 20% from a previous low point. Bulls charge forward, and that is exactly what happens during these longer, sustained periods of returns. As you have seen in an earlier graphic, the "bulls" outpace the "bears," but if you are not prepared and/or not protected, the timing of when you retire and when that intersects with one of these market trends can dictate what type of retirement you will experience.

One of the things you will not see in the above graphics is the minutiae of smaller time segments. If you are retired, and starting to withdraw money from your account, you can run out of money too soon even if you don't experience a bear market. Smaller losses and lower gains early in a retirement can erode your retirement prematurely.

As we illustrated earlier with *sequence of returns risk*, you can experience a period of attractive overall yields, while still running out of money too soon. This has everything to do with how early in your retirement those losses come (and yes, the severity of the losses can worsen the negative impact).

So, be on guard for bear markets, but more importantly, be prepared for any losses or smaller gains early in retirement. One thing we know about a market-driven retirement is that there will be peaks and valleys. Some instances can result in a less-than-desirable, if not completely wretched retirement! Using an FIA can eliminate that part of the rollercoaster ride that you don't want to experience.

Pushing Forward Back

During the first half of our country's history, we were much more tied to agricultural and manufacturing output, and our volume of stock trading was much lower. Much of this output was a direct result of World War I and II. What is my point? When we look at what the stock market has done over the past 100 years, it does not necessarily indicate what the stock market will do over the next 100 years. Early in the 20th century, a drought or shortage of raw materials for steel production could cause a market slide. Today, the market can swing because of the threat of a virus or potential banking collapse created by overselling of derivatives. These are two starkly different problems and indicate that the future market issues might very well be something we don't see coming. The next two graphics show the top 50 companies by sector in 1917 compared to 2017. Notice that the top-ranking sector from 1917 (Steel Production) isn't even in the top 50 in 2017, and the same with the top sector from 2017 (Tech), which wasn't even a thought in 1917.

The Largest Firms by Sector, 1917 (Asset Value in $Millions)

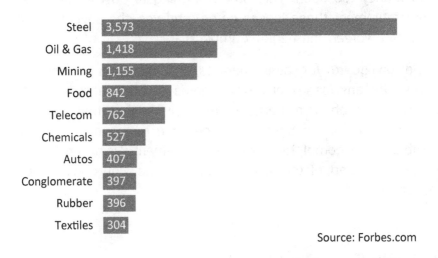

Sector	Value
Steel	3,573
Oil & Gas	1,418
Mining	1,155
Food	842
Telecom	762
Chemicals	527
Autos	407
Conglomerate	397
Rubber	396
Textiles	304

Source: Forbes.com

We just don't know what the future holds with the U.S. stock market, but it always behooves us to take a look at our history and see if there is any correlation we can derive, even if that correlation is the repeated lesson that markets go up and they go down. As for what the history of the United States and what that

The Largest Firms by Sector, 2017 (Asset Value in $Millions)

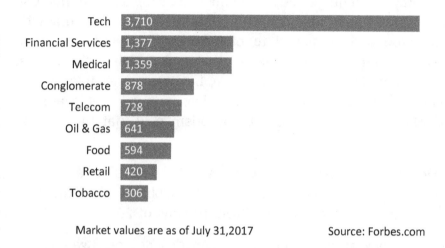

Sector	Value
Tech	3,710
Financial Services	1,377
Medical	1,359
Conglomerate	878
Telecom	728
Oil & Gas	641
Food	594
Retail	420
Tobacco	306

Market values are as of July 31,2017   Source: Forbes.com

can tell us about the future? Well, it is certainly difficult to know, because so much of what created our economic momentum in the 20th century is left in the 20th century.

There is, of course, the Great Depression of 1929 to 1933, where economic policy and labor laws culminated into the worst economic downfall in our history. It was difficult to recover from because of the massive job loss. Loss of income and our country's GDP dropped by approximately 50%. Fortunately, many of the policies and laws that created and exaggerated the crash of 1929 have since been fixed.

World War I and II both dropped the market initially, but during the recovery that followed, the market enjoyed a period of sustained growth. However, since the Korean War in the early 1950s, there has not been, and will most likely not be, the same sort of total war as we saw in the first half of the 20th century. War is a terrible thing, please understand that, but winning world wars does have a very positive outcome on the victors' economy. That alone is a striking difference in what we saw in the 20th century that we will most likely not see in the 21st century.

In 1987, "Black Monday" saw a crash that represented the largest single-day percentage drop of market loss up to that point in history. This programmatic error, that allowed for a dramatic initial drop and continued to plummet by fear, has now been prevented with "circuit breakers" that kick in when the market drops a certain percentage at once, but what other bugs in the system have yet to be detected? Also, how vulnerable are the markets to cyberattack or cyberterrorism now that they are all 100% electronic?

Moving into the 21st century, we see the rise of stranger and unforeseen crises, such as the "dot-com" bubble in 2001, the bank collapse of 2008, and now the Covid-19 virus of 2020.

When we look at what caused these market declines, we can see just how fragile the market can be. Some are caused by overall recessions in the economy, and others are caused by single events that strike fear in the market.

The bear market in March 2020 was recovered from quickly, but this immediate recovery might be standing up the market because of historically low yields in the bond markets. When investors, institutional and personal alike, can't get any yield in the bond market, they continue to pour money into the stock market. In fact, 2020 was a record-breaking year for valuation of *initial public offerings* (IPOs). In 2020, there were higher IPO evaluations than ever before (breaking the record set in 1999 at the peak of the "dot-com" boom). This can only be explained by the desire for investors to find some sort of return for their investment, even if it comes at the cost of overpaying for stocks. What will happen when interest rates eventually rise, and bond yields become attractive again? How far will the market drop?

There is an index that was created by Robert Shiller, known as the *Shiller Ratio*, which measures the price multiple paid for a stock. Notice how high the ratio is in 2020 compared to historical values. If we understand that 2001 represents an ignorance on how to price dot-com companies and know that it was followed by a very drastic bear market where these inflated values were corrected, then we can start to piece together some ominous signs that show where we might be headed.

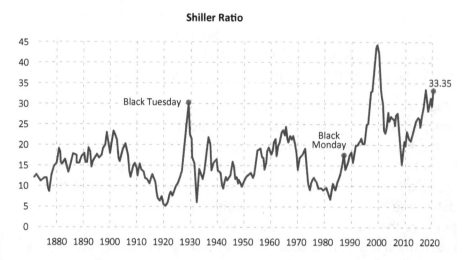

Shiller Ratio

Am I predicting a market crash? No. What I am doing is looking at the factors that can make up a market crash and noticing that some of them are here and now. This means that those who are preparing for retirement or in retirement need to heed these warning signs and protect a portion of their retirement. Remember, it doesn't need to be a dramatic bear market to affect one's retirement. Even a market correction of 10% or 20% could completely change the type of retirement you'll have. How much someone needs to protect differs widely because everyone's situation is unique, but regardless of your situation, no one wants to be caught unprepared. Once again, an FIA can offer the perfect balance of protection if the markets do slide, with attractive upside gain potential that won't leave you stranded if the markets continue to climb. And remember, once you activate lifetime income from an annuity, your payments are guaranteed no matter what the market does!

America the Young

Our country is the greatest country in the world, but it is also one of the youngest. In its short history, it has been the lynchpin for winning two world wars on its industrial might, and it is the birthplace of massive innovation, including Ford Motor Co., Boeing, Microsoft, Amazon, Dell Computers, IBM, and many, many more. But does our history dictate what our future will look like?

When we evaluate an investment, part of what we look at is how it has performed and use that as an indicator of how it will perform in the future. For those who are educated in stock evaluation, they know that relying on this metric alone can be dangerous. There are many other factors and far too many unforeseen events that will determine what the future will bring. So, why do we put so much faith in the U.S. markets as a whole? Many of the events that created such a strong U.S. stock market for the past 100 years are no longer a certainty in the future.

Rather than looking at the history of the U.S. markets as a gauge for what the future will look like, we can gain some potential insight as to what the future of the U.S. stock market might be by looking to countries that are older than ours and seeing how they have fared.

Starting with the French stock market, the *Cotation Assistée en Continu 40* is an index that tracks the 40 most significant stocks among the 100 largest market caps on the Euronext Paris (the French stock exchange). We see that it has yet to recover from its all-time high dating back to the very beginning of the 21st century. This is a period of more than twenty years. Could you imagine trying to plan your retirement based on expectations of future growth if you retired at that time? What assurances do we have in the United States that we won't experience anything similar, or even worse than what France has endured?

Cotation Assistée en Continu 40

Source: TradingEconomics.com

Now, let's look at the oldest market of them all, the Amsterdam stock market. Once again, we can see that it reached an all-time high shortly after the year 2000, which it has never been able to reach in the twenty years since. What economic factors have led to this? Perhaps the continued promulgation of increased unemployment benefits, stimulus checks, and bail-out money during the 2020 pandemic could lead to just such a decline in the United States?

Amsterdam Exchange

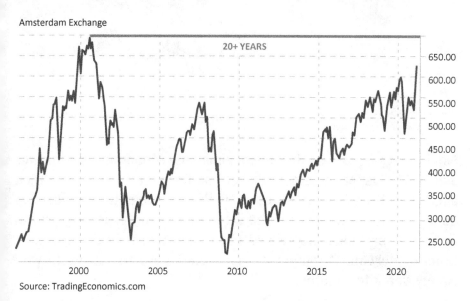

Source: TradingEconomics.com

A country that was ravaged by unemployment, Italy, has also been hit hard when it comes to the performance of the stock market. We, too, in the United States, have seen unemployment rise to uncomfortable levels. Could we expect the same trend for our stock market in the future?

Below are the historical values of the Italian stock exchange, the *Borsa Italiana.* You can see how it has dropped dramatically since its high in 2000 and has struggled to return half of its value over two decades later. Italy has a history of failed economic policies and large unemployment droughts, especially in the agricultural sector, which is different from the United States, but this does not make us immune from some of these similar impacts in the future.

FTSE Milano Italia Borsa

Source: TradingEconomics.com

Finally, let's look at the once-dominant economic superpower, Japan. The Japanese stock market has finally recovered from their all-time high back in 1996, but it took just about twenty years to do so. For those Japanese who were retiring and expecting growth from their portfolio, they would have been tragically disappointed. Unfortunately, most retirement plans don't have the ability to wait twenty years for returns.

Nikkei

Source: TradingEconomics.com

I do think it is important to recognize that the United States represents the premier free-market economy in the world. We have a stock market that reflects an economy built on capitalism, and I believe it can weather a storm better than any other country, but we are not exempt. What will the future hold? Will there be another terrorist attack? Perhaps another pandemic? Could there be a cyber-crime for the ages that shuts down our markets altogether? Maybe there will be an earthquake that hits Seattle or a tsunami that wipes out California. Any one of these events could mean disaster to the economy and the stock market, and we have no way of predicting or preventing them. Wouldn't it make sense to have some of your retirement protected from this? An FIA does just that and can be the portion of your retirement nest-egg that helps you sleep at night. It is a retirement tool that allows you to enjoy the retirement rollercoaster, not dread it.

CHAPTER IX

WARNING! DRAWBACKS TO FIAs

Not for Your Growth Phase

There are FIAs that allow for multiple premiums to be placed into the annuity over time. In my professional opinion, these are vehicles that one should not invest in if they are looking to optimize their returns during their growth phase of their financial life cycle.

I have previously explained the power of dollar cost averaging (DCA) and the value that one achieves from investing into the stock market over a sustained period of time. In short, having a market with volatility is a good thing while accumulating wealth. When the market is down, your monthly investment will garner more shares of that stock or fund and when it eventually recovers, you will achieve a multiple on your growth.

Without getting too complicated, any FIA that allows for multiple premiums to be placed into it must attempt to predict the future price of call options and the amount of yield from the underlying investments of the company to provide the guarantees and expected performance of the annuity. Obviously, the annuity company doesn't know what the future holds, so it is having to take on extra risk by doing so. Who do you think ultimately pays for that risk? You do. Annuity companies are going to offer very conservative caps, participation rates, and spreads when issuing a multi-premium annuity because they are having to bet on the future, and they need to account for potentially adverse climates.

When Congress passed the SECURE Act in 2019, it pushed annuities into the mainstream when it comes to defined contribution plans (i.e., 401(k)), and this is a good thing for those who are getting ready to retire and need to protect their nest-egg or generate lifetime income. However, when these contribution options are used during the growth phase, they can negatively affect the account by stunting the growth. Yes, while accumulating your retirement, you can actually be too conservative!

According to Plan Sponsor Council of America, less than 10% of defined contribution plans allow for annuity contributions inside the plan, and this is as much a reflection of the lack of desire for administrators to want them in the plan (remember, they don't want an insurance company to hold the money) as it is the lack of ability for annuities to work inside a defined contribution plan. As we will discuss in this chapter, annuity companies need to have assurance that your money will stay with them for longer, predictable time horizons. To do so, they normally have some sort of liquidity limitation and a surrender schedule to penalize excessive withdrawals. Obviously, these two things can't exist inside a defined contribution plan (at least not in the same way they do outside of one), so the very fiber in which and how annuities are built is stressed when offered inside a 401(k) (or other defined contribution plan).

What do I recommend? Simply put, I would avoid multi-premium fixed indexed annuities. This normally coincides with someone's age and where they are in their financial life cycle, but if someone is in a place where they need to accumulate money through regular and consistent contributions, then an FIA is not the preferred vehicle. Even if you are older and/or conservative and don't want to have your money fluctuate dramatically in value, there are still plenty of conservative funds and exchange traded funds (ETFs) that can stay relatively steady in their value. This also allows for the additional benefit of receiving any dividends that might be paid so you can capture additional upside while accumulating during the growth phase of your financial life cycle.

My hope in explaining this is that those who read it understand that I am truly approaching this agnostically, and I am not someone who simply has an agenda to sell more annuities. As I will explain in the last chapter, there are many ways to achieve the same or similar goals but using annuities during your accumulation phase is not optimal and should be avoided.

Understand Surrender Charges

What exactly are these surrender charges I have been mentioning? As my mother always said, "If something is too good to be true, then it's not true!" This is sage advice, and when we look at the seven great benefits that FIAs offer, we must assume there is some sort of catch. That catch is something called a surrender schedule. What a surrender schedule does is create a rule that limits the amount of liquidity that an annuity owner has while their money is in the annuity.

Here's how it works. The annuity has a certain number of years that it is designed to hold the money, let's say ten. Coincidentally, that number is usually in the name of the annuity. If we see an annuity called the "Best Annuity 10," then that "10" at the end of the name indicates the surrender period. During this period, the amount of money that can be withdrawn from the annuity is limited to a certain percentage each year. A common percentage we see in the industry is 10%, but there are some that allow less and some that allow more. So, if we have an annuity with $100,000 inside it, and the contract allows for a 10% annual withdrawal, then we can take out $10,000.

Year	Surrender Charge
0	8.5%
1	7.5%
2	6.5%
3	5.5%
4	5.0%
5	4.0%
6	2.0%
7	0.0%

The above graphic shows an example of a surrender schedule. The longer the annuity is owned, the smaller the surrender fee is. Remember, this charge is only for funds taken out *above and beyond* the allowed percentage each year (often 10%). Required minimum distributions (RMDs) can never be penalized by the annuity company but can count toward your annual withdrawal limit.

There is a quick field test you should do. Ask yourself how much money you plan on needing each year. If you need to take out more than 10%, then you don't have a retirement plan that would work! In fact, if you need to take out more than 5%, you still don't have a retirement plan that would work. In 1994, William Bengen, in a Trinity University study, calculated that in any historical thirty-year look back period of the U.S. stock market, a traditional bond/stock portfolio would survive if you took out no more than 4% per year (understand that he didn't account for advisory fees, and yields were much higher when the study was done, so the true amount is probably closer to 3%). This was coined as the SAFEMAX, or *safest-maximum* amount you can withdraw per year. So, if you followed that 4% withdrawal maximum per year, you would be well within annuities' withdrawal limits, and the "lack of liquidity" would be a none issue. Taking out more than what is allowed by an annuity each year from your retirement account would be the equivalent of pressing the self-destruct button, because no retirement can withstand double-digit withdrawals year over year.

Market Value Adjustments

We have explained that annuities are structured and require predictability. That is why they are longer in term (seven to fifteen years normally) and have a surrender schedule. But what if someone does want to cancel their annuity early, or take out more than the allowed percentage in a year? This is where *market value adjustments* (MVA) come in.

An MVA is basically an adjustment, positive or negative, that is applied when the contract is either surrendered early, or when a withdrawal is made beyond the allowed amount for that year. This adjustment is based on the 10-year Treasury bond rates. If the rates were higher when the annuity was purchased than when it was surrendered, the client would get money credited *back* to them. If the Treasury bond rates were lower when the annuity was purchased, then the MVA is negative and the client can have money subtracted from their surrender value.

I believe it is important to note two things. First, MVAs shouldn't happen. Why? Because if you have planned correctly, you should not need to take out an excessive amount or surrender your annuity early. Instances where you must do this, such as death, critical illness, or terminal illness, are usually accounted for in the annuity contract and the surrender fees and MVA are waived.

Second, the yield curve is very flat, and the forecast for yields isn't predicting any sort of drastic change in the future. We are in unprecedented times when it comes to historically low yields. If you purchase an annuity in 2020, yields almost have to be higher in the future, which would result in a negative MVA if surrendered early. However, the more oppressive prediction points to yields staying low for a long, long time. This would essentially result in a neutral MVA situation—one where a small deviation from the current value could maintain for years and possibly even decades.

Annuity companies would argue (and I would agree) that MVAs are good for the consumer, because the MVA protects the insurance company from having to sell inferior yielding bond investments before they are matured and lose money. MVAs allow annuity companies the ability to offer higher rates and more participation to the consumer because they don't have to hedge against this sort of short-sale. This does make sense. If you purchased a ten-year fixed indexed annuity, the annuity company will align certain investments that match up to that term (ten years). If you surrendered it six years into the contract, the annuity company now must sell those ten-year investments on the secondary market. Those investments are mostly bonds, and if the yield from those bonds is higher than what can be purchased currently, then they will have no trouble selling them and will be able to sell them at a premium, which will pass on to the consumer. This is known as a positive MVA. But if the yields from those original ten-year investments are lower than what can be purchased at the time of the annuity surrender, the annuity company will have to sell them at a discount and recoup the difference from the consumer.

So, be aware of MVAs and make sure you plan accordingly. If looking at the purchase of an annuity, make sure you check and see under what situations the MVA and/or surrender charges would be waived.

CHAPTER X

TO ALL AGENTS, ADVISORS, AND CLIENTS

Pick A Game Plan

I have always been a huge fan of football. Growing up in Seattle, I saw the Seahawks emerge from perennial losers to Super Bowl victors. I've watched many teams, at all levels, and admired what it is that makes them winners. What I've learned is that it's not the offense you run that makes you a winner, it's the buy-in from the team and the commitment to the plan that makes you a winner.

This rule also applies to finding success with retirement planning. Yes, there are certain obvious things that should always be avoided. For instance, you would never expose all your retirement savings to one single stock, just like you wouldn't run a quarterback sneak every play in football, but essentially, all *viable* plans can work. The client and the advisor or agent need to understand the plan and stick to the plan for it to succeed.

Perhaps you have a retirement game plan that is more conservative. It involves a lot more bond-based funds and maybe a mix of fixed and indexed annuities. Maybe you have a more aggressive plan that has a stable of hand-picked stocks and funds. Either of these plans—and many variations in between—can work, so long as they are forged with a pragmatic base and all parties stick to the plan.

Investing and finances can be tricky to figure out. If you are looking to research a plan for its legitimacy, you can often get paralyzed with the back-and-forth opinions and arguments both for and against the plan in question. Unfortunately, these arguments are often formed on either side based on the compensation that would be derived from the respective plan. In reality, there is very little black and white, and most of all, no one knows for sure exactly what the future will hold. This research leads to constant indecision and lack of action. It is, by default, the worst way to prepare for and execute a retirement plan. It would be the equivalent of not being able to decide which offense you want your team to run, so you just don't pick an offense. How is this redressed? Just like a Super Bowl winning team, it's not the decision to be more run-based or pass-based. It's not the formation choice of having two running backs or one, or four receivers or two tight ends. No, it all comes down to the buy-in and the decision to commit to and stick with the plan!

Clients, when you are working with your financial specialist(s) and you understand the goal and how you are going to reach it, at some point you need to take action. A good plan will always be reviewed and changed accordingly, but without action, no plan can succeed.

Agents and advisors, when you are working with your clients, create a plan that best suits their needs, not yours. Involve others where you require additional expertise. You need to have confidence in working with the products and concepts that you know and understand, and when you know those products and concepts will work, avoid getting distracted chasing down countless other variations or hearsay that doesn't move you forward. Just like your clients, indecision and lack of action are what will sink the plan foremost, so plan accordingly and then take action. Annual reviews and continued education will help keep the plan on track.

Same Team

Within all aspects of financial planning, you have competition. Competition is good! Without competition, there would not be companies and individuals out there looking for ways to earn your business by creating better solutions for less cost. This is capitalism at its finest. However, when that competition starts to take the shape of slander and greed, then it hurts everyone involved.

There are constant battles between those who do sell annuities and those who don't. Most allegiances can be traced back to how that specific professional is licensed and how they get paid. For agents of broker dealers, they might present a client with a variable annuity to accomplish the client's goals instead of a fixed indexed annuity because the latter of those two options would no longer be counted in their assets under management. Conversely, an insurance-only licensed agent, who is not legally able to sell a variable annuity, might push for an FIA and encourage a client not to purchase that variable annuity. Again, this can be traced back to the fact that the insurance agent is licensed to sell the FIA and will receive a commission for the sale of the FIA. Who is right in this situation?

As I've stated in this book, I am not a fan of most variable annuities because of their high fees and lower guarantees when compared to other forms of annuities, but more importantly, I encourage advisors and agents to remember to keep the focus on the client and not on the competition.

What I have seen so many times is that one party shifts from explaining the advantages of their plan to attacking the disadvantages of the other plan. This often escalates to the point of aggravation and involves absolutes. Absolutes are when an advisor or agent states, "I would never purchase one of those!" Or, "Buying that is a dumb idea!" The variations of these slanderous salvos are as long as this book. This is what needs to end. Both securities (Securities & Exchange Commission) products and insurance products have merit. If not, they wouldn't be allowed in our highly regulated country. In the majority of instances, an optimal retirement will include both.

I believe the source of this contention has to do with the polarizing licensing requirements and needs to be resolved through teamwork and partnerships. Fixed indexed annuities are an extremely capable and valuable tool for retirees, so disputing the purchase of one because it doesn't count as assets under management (AUM) for an advisor is only hurting our clients. For those agents on the other side, who tout the stock market as "gambling" and "high risk," they need to understand that the market provides an excellent source of inflation protection, long-term growth potential, capital gains advantages, and excellent dividend options. Yes, the market has risk, and a retirement plan without protection is unprotected, but this is not as polarizing as advisors and agents sometimes make it.

For consumers who are reading this, play your part. Know that both sides have value and encourage your advisors and agents to work together. I encourage you to request a couple different plans, and then, especially if they both appear worthy of consideration, ask the two advisors or agents to work together. This request can keep both parties honest and create a lot of goodwill amongst all.

Lastly, remember the connection. It is important to work with others with whom we have a connection. I want to clarify that I don't mean association, I mean connection. An association is often how financial advisors get "assigned" to us. If our parents used a certain financial advisor, we now are expected to use them because of that association. Or, if we practice a certain religious faith, we are expected to use a certain company because of our association. When it comes to association and selecting an advisor, it's a bad idea.

I am talking about a connection. A connection might be someone you have known for years, it might be someone you have an association with, or it might be someone you just recently met. For the same reasons we know someone could be the "right one" when we are dating, a connection with someone is something we feel, not something we derive from logic. It is important to have a connection with your agent because they will be the one who you need to trust and communicate with, and they will need to relate and empathize with you for the outcome to be optimal.

For advisors and agents, this idea of connection should be mutual. If you have a client who would make for a good commission, but you find yourself tolerating their personality and not enjoying it or at least appreciating it, then you will not be as effective as you need to be. You are better off allowing them to work with someone else.

In both instances, this takes a bit of maturity to diagnose properly. For me, personally, I know that there were two traits that I displayed that made me not a good connection for some people. Those traits were, first, my tendency to become a bit wound-up, and second, my explanations sometimes turn into long-winded, educational filibusters. Both traits I have worked on for years to curtail and I believe I've improved dramatically, but be that as it may, there will be certain personalities that I am not a good fit with. If you lack the maturity to be honest in assessing who you are, and what type of personalities you get along with, then you are literally asking to have a much more stressful and far less productive time when it comes to financial planning.

Enjoy the Ride

Retirement can be a rollercoaster. Are you ready to enjoy the ride? What makes a rollercoaster fun is the mystery of what the next turn will be, and what it will feel like, while knowing you are safe. Retirement is only done once—it is a single-use ticket and you certainly do not know what the next climb, dip, or bend in the tracks is going to feel like. That can be exhilarating, but only if you have that sense of security. FIAs can provide that security, while still allowing you to feel the ride. We have reviewed what retirement has meant to generations before us. We have learned as best we can what retirement will be moving forward. We realize there are numerous challenges, and everyone's experience will be different. Most importantly of all, we have learned that we must have a plan if we are going to enjoy the ride. So, make that commitment today. Start or refine your plan based on what you have learned in this book and make sure you are doing everything you can to get the most enjoyment out of this ride!

CPSIA information can be obtained
at www.ICGtesting.com
Printed in the USA
LVHW111353180821
695584LV00014B/195

9 781737 279136